CW01202511

# Oneness

## *The Dynamics of Monasticism*

*Edited by*

Stephen Platten

scm press

© The Contributors 2017

Published in 2017 by SCM Press
Editorial office
3rd Floor, Invicta House,
108–114 Golden Lane,
London EC1Y 0TG, UK

www.scmpress.co.uk

SCM Press is an imprint of Hymns Ancient & Modern Ltd
(a registered charity)

Hymns Ancient & Modern® is a registered trademark of
Hymns Ancient & Modern Ltd 13A Hellesdon Park Road,
Norwich, Norfolk NR6 5DR, UK

British Library Cataloguing in Publication data

A catalogue record for this book is available
from the British Library
978 0 334 05532 7

Typeset by Manila Typesetting
Printed and bound by
CPI Group (UK) Ltd

For
Brother Harold Palmer,
whose vision and commitment inspired
the writing of these essays

# Contents

# CONTENTS

# List of Contributors

Justin Welby is Archbishop of Canterbury.

Diarmaid MacCulloch is Professor of the History of the Church at the University of Oxford.

Stephen Platten is an assistant bishop in the dioceses of London, Southwark and Newcastle, chairman of Hymns Ancient and Modern, and chairman of the governors of the Anglican Centre in Rome. He was formerly the Archbishop of Canterbury's Secretary for Ecumenical Affairs, Dean of Norwich and Bishop of Wakefield.

George Guiver CR is Superior of the Community of the Resurrection, and his writings include *Company of Voices* (1988 and 2000), *Pursuing the Mystery* (1996 and 2016) and *Vision upon Vision* (2009).

Sarah Foot is the Regius Professor of Ecclesiastical History at Christ Church, Oxford. She has published extensively on the early English Church, including *Veiled Women* (2 vols, 2000) and *Monastic Life in Anglo-Saxon England c. 600–900* (2006) and has written a life of *Æthelstan: The First King of England* (2011). She is currently starting work on a biography of the Venerable Bede.

Petà Dunstan is a Fellow of St Edmund's College, Cambridge. She has written on different aspects of Anglican religious life, including monographs on Anglican Franciscans (*This Poor Sort*, 1997) and Benedictines (*The Labour of Obedience*, 2009). She is also the editor of the *Anglican Religious Life Year Book*.

**Andrew Louth FBA** is Professor Emeritus of Patristic and Byzantine Studies at the University of Durham, archpriest of the Russian Orthodox Diocese of Sourozh (Moscow Patriarchate) and rector of the Orthodox parish in Durham. He is the author of several books and many articles, including *Origins of the Christian Mystical Tradition: Plato to Denys* (2nd edition, 2006), and most recently *Modern Orthodox Thinkers: From the Philokalia to the Present* (2015).

**Nicholas Alan Worssam** (Brother Nicholas SSF) has been a member of the Anglican religious community, the Society of Saint Francis, since 1995. Most of his time in community has been spent at Glasshampton Monastery in Worcestershire, where he is currently the Guardian. He has also spent some years at a Franciscan hermitage in South Yorkshire with another SSF brother, and delights in long retreats in Europe and the Far East.

**Dom Xavier Perrin** is the abbot of the Benedictine community of Quarr Abbey on the Isle of Wight (Solesmes Congregation), where he arrived in 2013. After reading literature and art at the Sorbonne, he joined the Benedictine abbey at Kergonan (France) in 1980. He studied theology in Solesmes, Fribourg and Munich. He was choirmaster in Kergonan for 16 years. He has taught Gregorian chant to many different groups and monastic communities in France and in England, specializing in the spirituality of the chant, and conducted a few CD recordings and concerts with the choirs of Kergonan and Quarr.

**Christopher Irvine** is the Canon Librarian and Director of Education at Canterbury Cathedral, and was formerly the Principal of the College of the Resurrection, Mirfield. He is a trustee of Art and Christianity Enquiry, and contributes to the teaching of the Liturgical Studies MA courses at Sarum College and the Mirfield Liturgical Institute. His previous publications include *The Use of Symbols in Worship* (2007) and *The Cross and Creation in Christian Liturgy and Art* (2013).

**Walter Herbert Ralph Pattisson** was educated at Ampleforth, and studied architecture at the University of Durham and at Newcastle

University. In his distinguished career he has won prizes for both ecclesiastical and domestic architecture. The first Hadrian RIBA Award was in recognition of his work on St Gregory's, South Shields. Ralph has been involved in the development of Shepherds Law from the outset of the building project, and in 2015 won the ACE Architecture Award for the Chapel.

**Rowan Williams** (The Rt Revd Lord Williams of Oystermouth) was Lady Margaret Professor of Divinity in the University of Oxford, Bishop of Monmouth, then successively Archbishop of Wales and Archbishop of Canterbury. He is currently Master of Magdalene College, Cambridge.

# Foreword

THE MOST REVEREND AND RIGHT
HONOURABLE THE LORD ARCHBISHOP
OF CANTERBURY JUSTIN WELBY

Prayer is the source and prayer changes everything.

Authentic religious life when it comes is always rooted in this source. And it is linked to what has gone before, drawing upon traditions ancient and modern but looking different because it is a new expression for new times.

In writing this volume, the contributors invite us to eavesdrop on a symphony. They draw together the chords of one remarkable and new expression of eremitic monastic life. They share the captivating story of 'Shepherds Law', the hermitage of St Mary and St Cuthbert perched in the Northumbrian hills. But behind Shepherds Law they skilfully tune our ears to hear its deep echoes. The echoes of Brother Harold's vision resonating with a dynamic, monastic tradition that spans continents and centuries. A vision in continuity with Francis, Benedict and the Northern saints. The contemplative call to the importance of silence, solitude in prayer and sheer obedience to God.

This is a collection of essays that illuminates in rich detail how monastics have struggled consciously, gracefully to shape their common life with Christ at the very centre in worship, architecture and community while living the tension of availability to the needs of the world and solitude. As George Guiver also writes, the ways in which religious communities have tried to: 'set a plumb line', a standard in liturgy and prayer for all, shine a light on the non-negotiables of Christian lives designed to serve God.

Brother Harold's very human example and the contributions that follow challenge our imaginations. Shepherds Law has taken time and struggle to be built in prayer, crafted in liturgy and shaped in stone. How might we in our own ordinary lives, patiently, lovingly build a breathing space for that dimension of God's grace to work in and through us? Where do we stand at the centre to face God? How does God call us to a place of transfiguration, to make Christ known and transform the world?

I thank God for the hermitage of St Mary and St Cuthbert and for this book. Through them both may many encounter the vibrant symbols, marker posts and reminders of God's covenant with us both now and in the years to come. May we be renewed in the mystery of God and see afresh the capacity of the human spirit to respond to Jesus in radical love.

# Prologue

## DIARMAID MACCULLOCH

Over the last year or two, Western society has been convulsed by a mood of revulsion at the ways in which we have organized our lives and our politics in recent decades. The mood has produced some strange political results, many of which might seem bizarre wrong turns and non sequiturs, but the mood cannot be ignored. Our leaders and the course our nations take have been weighed in the balance and found wanting, and the result is much angry noise and division. By contrast, in one remote and beautiful part of our country, there is a place which reminds us that there are more positive ways of turning our everyday assumptions inside out: ways of being human which draw on centuries of spiritual history, to bring balance, sanity and reverence to wider society, drawing on the energy of silence and prayer. The essays in this volume introduce the reader to a remarkable experiment in contemplation, which is no withdrawal from the world and which is not afraid to combine the ascetic with the aesthetic; the contributors place the experience of one spiritual venture into a much wider historical setting. You will learn here of the hospitality of Shepherds Law: its hospitality to those who seek peace, its hospitality to Christian traditions of both East and West, and its hospitality to a still wider world of divine contemplation. In a time when traditional religion often seems to have lost its self-confidence and its power to compel, here is a still small voice to provide energy and hope.

# PART I

# Setting the Scene

# Introduction

## STEPHEN PLATTEN

If you make your way to the hermitage of St Mary and St Cuthbert at Shepherds Law, leaving the Eglingham road and striking south-west up the hill, you will pass a disused quarry, now prodigiously concealed by undergrowth. It was from this quarry that the stone for the eighteenth-century folly farm at Shepherds Law was cut, much of which has now been reused in the buildings of the hermitage. It has literally been born of the buildings of the earth of Northumberland – indeed there are even fragments of brick from the seashore at Lindisfarne, further adding to the range of the Northumbrian landscape out of which the hermitage has been hewn and fashioned. This image, however, can be further extended. The views from the hermitage, as breathtaking as any in England, look northwards down Glendale towards the Lammermuir Hills in the Scottish borderlands. Here lie the ruins of the great border abbeys: Melrose, established originally by St Aidan and rebuilt later as a Cistercian house; Kelso, a Tironensian abbey; Dryburgh, the home of a Premonstratensian community and finally Jedburgh, where Augustinian canons had established a monastery.

It was at Melrose that Cuthbert received his training as a monk under the Abbot Boisil (modern day St Boswell, as in the border village of that name). Hidden from view behind Ros Castle and then the Kyloe Hills but no distance from Shepherds Law is the Holy Island of Lindisfarne. While it is impossible for us to appreciate the culture of seventh-century Northumbria 'enchanted' by a belief in humanity's utter dependence on God, nonetheless the atmosphere and landscape of Northumbria still breathe a far richer feeling of this than is appreciable in other parts of England.[1] Indeed, spreading one's net wider into the southern parts of ancient Northumbria will capture Whitby, Ripon and Lastingham among the early sites and then Fountains, Rievaulx and Byland among the great twelfth-century flowering of the Benedictine and Cistercian foundations. Standing alongside this are other sites traditionally associated with the seventh- and eighth-century renaissance of Christianity in north-east England and southern Scotland, as we now know them. On Inner Farne and Coquet Island there were hermitages traditionally associated with Cuthbert, and at Warkworth is a later hermitage cut out of the rock on the River Coquet. Not far from Holburn near Belford is the so-called St Cuthbert's Cave.

It is almost as if the monastic tradition is there within the soil. Its Northumbrian roots lie both within community but also in the solitary life, and indeed that mixture of these traditions described as the skete (tiny monasteries committed to the contemplative life). Mountgrace Priory – also in North Yorkshire and thus ancient Northumbria – offers a rare example of the Carthusian pattern where monks lived much of their life as independent souls but who also came together for corporate worship. It is out of this rich monastic soil that the hermitage at Shepherds Law has grown. This volume is neither a 'festschrift' to Shepherds Law, nor simply a description of how this one hermitage came to be. Instead, while celebrating the extraordinary countercultural establishment of the hermitage, these essays seek to indicate how this is a living, developing, flourishing expression of gospel life in a very different Northumbria from that of the seventh and eighth centuries, the time of Paulinus, Aidan, Cuthbert, Wilfred and Hilda, and in a contemporary society and Church very different from theirs.

If any persuasion is necessary in indicating how such a life still flourishes, there have been two very modern pointers to just one of the values that underpins the monastic life; that is, the significance of silence. Every five years or so, the Royal Institute of British Architects with Art and Christian Enquiry sponsor a prize for the best piece of ecclesiastical architecture to emerge during that period. The 2015 prize was divided between two joint winners, the new Quaker Centre at Kingston-upon-Thames and the chapel at Shepherds Law. Both places are dedicated to a committed and serious valuing of silence. Both very different patterns of observance spring from a response to the Christian gospel. At just this same time, Professor Diarmaid MacCulloch, the distinguished historian of the Reformation period, presented his Gifford Lectures also on *silence* within the Christian tradition.[2] Amid all the clamour of mobile telephones, the booming of rock music from open-top cars and even the amplifiers broadcasting the music of Christian rock bands in worship, the 'still small voice' continues to find its place.

The 'oneness' of the title picks up a key monastic theme: the term 'monk' is thought to derive from the Greek *monos*, meaning 'one'. The religious brother or sister is single, unmarried and pursues singleness of heart, all energies being directed one way; they embrace solitude, whether in community or in isolation; they seek to be at one with God; and they pray for the unity of all things, not least the unity of the Church, a central theme at Shepherds Law and indeed within all contemporary monasticism.

This selection of essays attempts to describe some elements of this lively tradition of monastic prayer and observance in our contemporary world. The background to Brother Harold Palmer and his establishment of the hermitage is traced and it is set in the context of the history recorded by Bede of the early apostles of the faith in Northumbria. The distinctive pattern of sketes is described as is the wider context of the monastic life and its positive challenge to our wider culture and to the Church more specifically. The challenges of today are not avoided or concealed, and instead monasticism is shown to be in dialogue with the contemporary Church, revealing ways in which each may need to examine themselves. The place of music, both in hymnody and Gregorian chant are described, as is the place of the liturgy itself and the crucial contribution of the saints. The buildings of the monastic tradition are an essential part of that life and also are included here. The present Archbishop of Canterbury has declared as one of the three main focuses of his archiepiscopate the importance of prayer and the various manifestations of the religious life.

These essays, then, are offered as a contemporary reflection and challenge on the Christian imperative to bring the gospel to all peoples and all nations. We complete this work at that season of Epiphany, when we particularly remember that part of our apostolic responsibilities.

## Notes

1 Cf. Rowan Williams's notes in his illuminating Introduction in Sister Benedicta Ward SLG and Rowan Williams (eds), *Bede's Ecclesiastical History of the English People: An Introduction and Selection*, London, Bloomsbury Continuum, 2012, pp. 1–27.

2 Diarmaid MacCulloch, *Silence: A Christian History*, London, Viking, 2013.

# I

# Religious Communities
# and Their Citizenship

## GEORGE GUIVER

Even after many years of decline, religious sisters and brothers are more numerous than most people realize, and their communities are beginning to find a new following as the world has unexpectedly started taking an interest in them. In many countries of the Western world, people are wanting to draw on the monastic tradition of life, in a phenomenon increasingly known as 'new monasticism'. New communities have been founded, which live the life in a way that is both traditional and also something new; and many small groups have formed, mainly dispersed rather than living together, whose members seek to live a form of the monastic life in the midst of the world. A number of seminal books in recent years have concluded as well that the future for Church and society must involve a serious engagement with monasticism.[1]

If we wish to understand a phenomenon, we need to discover what lies at its roots. In human psychology, for instance, or in situations that arise in politics, or in plants themselves, we can almost say the roots are everything. Scripture has a lot to say on this theme, especially in its repeated reference to the human heart as the place of truth about a human being. Heart, roots, deepest sources: the essence of who we are, and the life that is in us, is powered by a drive that springs from our depths.

In March 2016 news media reported that a crowd at Leicester football stadium became so excited that one roar caused a tremor measured a mile away at 0.03 on the Richter scale. That kind of vital energy surges up from people's profoundest core. Large enterprises such as professional football matches rely on such deep energy – without it everything flags or becomes mediocre, for people's hearts are not ultimately in it. In art there is something similar – the greatness of a painting doesn't come from the artist's technique, or ideas, or planning or forethought – it exerts itself with an energetic sovereignty coming forth from an inner life.

In this respect, how do the churches look today? Can we detect such energy surging from a vibrant core? It is certainly around in pockets, and yet pockets can't make a seamless robe, a corporate, unstoppable *whoosh*. The Church can produce plenty of cheerfulness, but as a corporate entity it hardly grabs attention through being shot through with a vital force impelling the whole project forward. If we were seeking an example comparable to the energy of a January sale, the Church would not immediately spring to mind as a place to look. The energetic places and people are there all right, but their potential effect on the body is muffled by a surrounding sea of half-life.

## The communist comparison

At this point a haunting picture rises up of the countries of the old Eastern Europe in the time of communism. The state ran everything you saw; everything was publicly owned; nothing was done properly. New housing had doors and plumbing that didn't work; shops were dowdy and service poor; seats collapsed in the new car you had waited years for; there was little incentive to do anything well, amid a prevailing sense that nothing mattered because it all belonged to everybody and nobody, and the ideals proclaimed by authority failed to convince. In Romania the dictator Nicolae Ceausescu appeared regularly on television haranguing workers who had produced shoddy goods, in a constant effort to stoke up enthusiasm in the face of apathy. There was a chronic lack of fit between what was claimed from above and what was true of people's inner convictions. Then you visited a monastery of monks or nuns – and you found by contrast a world where everything worked. The place would be run with such excellence that you wondered if you had moved into another income-bracket, while in fact this effect was simply due to people there being committed to the best. Here was something to die for, and it came not from people being badgered to do better, but from Christianity's deep sources.

It might seem unexpected to compare communist Romania with the contemporary churches in the rich West, but there are close similarities: for many people a lack of will to own the enterprise; not all of your heart is in it, and you have insufficient motivation to give your all. In the Romania of those times there was no root-energy, no driving force motivating the whole population to throw themselves into the national endeavour, but rather a fruitless process of the few trying to exhort people from the top downwards. The ideology didn't hold water compared with, say, the 'ideology' of the government in wartime Britain under Churchill. The churches differ from the communist state in that there are many places where there is life and commitment and hope for the future. That has to be said and given thanks for. The situation is patchy, however, and patchiness reduces the potential of everything. This is everywhere evident in the area of the inner life. Many if not most laity struggle with prayer, or are going about it in too isolated a way; and the situation of the clergy is hardly less parlous. All of us need to be able to speak to others about God, confident in our relationship with him, but if the truth were told, that kind of confidence is far from universal. When I was a curate I neglected my prayer life until it was non-existent. Then one day I found myself in a front room speaking with a man who had just been bereaved. All that I had picked up as a child in the parish, and lived in my early adult life came back to me, and I knew that I needed to speak of God, and I couldn't without feeling a fraud. That drove me back to prayer.

There is for some a bewailing of things we want to believe but which elude us; and in the church culture there is a danger of being all singing and dancing but with thin spiritual resources. Because of this patchy spiritual landscape, the places that are spiritually well-grounded and flourishing cannot reach their full potential. There is the image of the coals in a roaring fire: if you take the coals out and set them separately in a row on the fender, you can watch them slowly go out. Only together can they create a lively fire in which an overplus of strong life is generated. However brightly some of its coals may burn, the whole body of the Church is not at present good at bringing them all together so that something else may happen which is more than the sum of the individual parts, a Church fully alive. The early Cistercian Baldwin of Ford said that the human heart is enlarged when it is unified.[2] An integrated person is one whose disparate parts have come together in a good focus, and an integrated Church would be the same. One of the great themes of monasticism is singleness of heart, where the focus on the one brings together the warring and jostling parts within us to a state of living, attentive oneness.

## Where does the energy come from?

The Christian faith in its early beginnings swept all before it. The lives of ordinary people in the Roman Empire of that time were precarious. There were the rich and powerful, and then everybody else. The rich despised people who worked with their hands. Even though they relied on the labours of ordinary people for their food, services and everything that needed doing for them, they despised them for the fact that they worked. The armies of slaves who built colossal buildings and ran them were routinely treated with unbelievable callousness. If they fell ill, for instance, it was normal simply to finish them off. Strangely for us, the pagan religions had no moral dimension. According to David Bentley Hart these religions showed a complete

> tolerance – without any qualms of conscience – of poverty, disease, starvation, and homelessness; of gladiatorial spectacle, crucifixion, the exposition of unwanted infants, or the public slaughter of war captives or criminals on festive occasions; of, indeed, almost every imaginable form of tyranny, injustice, depravity, or cruelty. The indigenous sects of the Roman world simply made no connection between religious piety and anything resembling a developed social morality.[3]

Into such a world came Christ's message that every human being was of infinite value in the sight of God, and we were to value one another in the same way. We belong to each other and are to love one another, because the dignity of every human being is incalculable. We cannot easily imagine the effect of this on people at the time. This thrilling new way of living so caught people's imagination that it worked its way through the whole of society, gradually sweeping all before it. Christianity at that time had an inner core of dynamic energy, an irresistible driving force at its heart, pumping life into all its parts: 'Love your neighbour, love your enemies, once you were no people, now you are God's people.' It brought a transformative earthquake into people's lives, an awareness that their whole situation was being stood on its head.

Energy always has a source, and the issue held before us here, as in 1970s Romania or the contemporary churches of the West, is precisely that of the *source*. The main role of monastic life is to stand at the source, to stand there pointing to it. Shepherds Law as a small monastic house plays its part in a much wider network of religious communities seeking to stand at the life-source of the faith. They may seem energetic or they may not, but that is not the point – their role is to be markers, reminders, standing largely silently, there at the source, and this is where this book needs to begin.

## Monasticism and the Church

This standing-at-the-source is bound up with identity. An example would be the family, which provides a secure setting for children to grow up. A healthy family imparts a sense of identity that most of the time is completely tacit. The child who is balanced, happy and making the most of her energy and gifts can be all of these things because of a tacit awareness of the family, which is central to her sense of who she is. Break-up of the family will often affect these things for the worse, not least the sense of who she is, for in the family we find significant foundations of our identity.

Tacit awareness of our belonging is important for us at many levels. A person in a dangerous situation in a foreign country can find psychological support in the simple knowledge that their nation is there, even if practical help is not readily possible. Once when preparing to smuggle documents about persecution out of Ceausescu's Romania, and in a highly nervous state, I was relieved on a visit to the British Embassy simply to hear ordinary English spoken by English people with their local accents, partly because it reminded me of who I was and of the things that counted. It came as a tonic at the right time. Tacit awareness of belonging is an essential ingredient in human flourishing and in having command of our lives.

We gain in a variety of ways from different kinds of corporate belonging. For instance, while membership of a regiment may bring benefits I have just mentioned, one particular thing it can provide is inspiration and pride. Membership of a charity working for the poor, on the other hand, can impart a strong sense of belief in what you are doing. In bringing together the energies of supporters of a football team, corporate belonging can satisfy the best, and the worst, of our tribal instincts. Particular kinds of human grouping contribute to human identity each in their own way.

This leads us to consider religious corporate identity: what we mean by the 'Church' can today take different forms, some of them wide of the mark. One common view is to see the Church as a human institution: it is set up and held in being by our own efforts, a pooling of the resources of people who happen to believe. The deepest resources of the faith lie in individual Christians and their relation to Scripture and the tradition; through their efforts, guided by the Holy Spirit, all of this is brought together in an organization which *we* create and *we* run. It is up to us to enable it to work. The Church according to this view is an organization with a task, an imperfect organization that needs continually to be challenged, tweaked and improved by means of free debate: a machine that can be made to work better so long as we tinker with it in the right way. This, the Church as a human organization, has its roots in the everyday world that is familiar to us and immediately corresponds to our sense of normality.

In a Church completely like this, monasticism could not exist. This view of a purely human organization fits with what is normal in our society, but religious communities stand apart from what counts as 'normal', from the ways of the world in which they are set. They choose to live without many freedoms, possibilities and facilities that are expected in contemporary life, and in the same way their understanding of the Church is different from a 'normal' contemporary understanding of it as a human organization to be 'managed'. In this they are not seeking to be different from their fellow-Christians in any way, but simply seeking to live the life of the gospel – something to which all Christians are called. The gospel which Jesus proclaims turns many things on their heads: the poor are fed while the rich are sent empty away, those who consider themselves first are made last, while the dregs of the earth are surprised to receive places of honour; life, freedom and joy come through a death on a cross.

Visual images can be a help in crystallizing concepts, and we could start here with a vision of a tree. Its strong, vigorous roots spread far and wide, while on its branches broad, shapely leaves shimmer with life. It is an exceedingly fine tree, but at the same time there is something so odd about it that we are stopped in our tracks – it commands our attention not only for its magnificence, but for the strange fact that it is upside-down; its roots go up into the clouds, while beautiful, rustling leaves brush the ground. This upside-down tree is the gospel, turning on its head the wisdom of this world in ways that often appear simply foolish.

In line with the principle that the gospel turns everything topsy-turvy, the Church as seen from the standpoint of religious communities has its roots not in the everyday world that is familiar to us, roots in the ground, so to speak, but in the air – it is rooted not in human endeavours to construct, manage and improve, but in the kingdom of heaven and the power and grace of God. Whether they be sisters and brothers working among the homeless in a big city, or monastics living a more enclosed contemplative life, the tacit awareness is of a Church that is only secondarily a human organization. This needs some explanation.

## A great throng

The Christian who prays never prays alone: all over the world there are people praying at the same time, with and for each other. St Cyprian of Carthage pointed out as early as the second century that the Lord's Prayer is in the plural – Christ did not tell us to pray 'my father in heaven . . . give me this day my daily bread . . .', but 'Our Father . . .'. This recognition that we are not alone when we pray can come as a revelation to many people who struggle with prayer. Ultimately for Christians there is no such thing as private prayer – prayer is something which holds us all together, in communication with each other as well as with God. This is not any old belonging with others, but a central peculiarity of the gospel. The sense of not being alone is a sense of being within the body of Christ. Jesus founded this body, he said he *is* it, and gives himself to us in it – a body in which there are many organs, each member contributing its particular part, but all cohering in the whole. Christ is the vine, we are the branches and the sap courses through every part. The Church also spans the divide of death, and in all our prayers we are united with the Church on earth and in heaven – most of the Church, like an iceberg, is invisible. But even here in this world much of the body of Christ is invisible to us: the Church in other parts of the world, other denominations and the various organs of the Church – we cannot see all of them at work, the tradition, the original context and significance of the Scriptures, much of the work going on even in our own neighbourhood. In a televised, digitized world which wants to see everything, the gospel holds before us the importance of living with an awareness of the invisible. This was felt to be sufficiently important to have its place in the Nicene Creed (whose original form reads: *we* believe . . .): '. . . Creator of all things, visible and invisible . . .' Here is the first great thing to grasp: the gospel calls us to a sense of belonging together with the whole of humanity, and within that to the body of Christ on earth and in heaven, eternally singing the New Song of Revelation, so that when we pray we tune into that new song, joined by an immeasurable chorus of voices, who are helping carry us, while we help carry them.

## One Church, one Lord

Despite human divisions, there are ultimately not many churches, but one great mystery, just as there are not many people at prayer, but one prayer encompassing all who engage in it. This sense of the Church universal has led communities to develop international connections, and many of their members to travel; the religious life has a different character in different countries and cultures, and in modern times the developing chemistry between them has been life-giving. It can even be said that if you believe in the Church in the way I have been describing, then if it is possible and will not undermine essential elements in your calling, you need nowadays to travel. Such travel not only creates friendships and forms of cooperation, but also encourages us to be supple, holding together, as we come to discover many variations on the same theme, and setting us free from thinking only in terms of our own limited culture and ways of believing and acting.

Not enough people know that religious communities exist in many if not most of the main churches of the Reformation. In Lutheranism there are strong communities, including female and male Benedictines, and in the Reformed churches (Calvinist/ Zwinglian) there are well-established communities in France, Switzerland and elsewhere. Regular international congresses including these, and Anglicans, Roman Catholics, Orthodox and others, have become, over the years, a privileged space for discovery of all that the communities have in common – much more than the things that divide them. It is a peculiar characteristic of Christianity to produce people urged to a vowed community life, and this life is an eloquent witness to the unity that already exists between the churches. There is among all these communities often a passion for the unity of the fragmented mystery of the Church, and a commitment to prayer for unity.

The propensity for travel, and for the bridging of boundaries, has meant that religious communities have been in the forefront of the quest for Christian unity, and as a result there are some monastic foundations which do not fit easily into any denomination, however firmly rooted they are in particular church structures. This is one of the foundational characteristics of Shepherds Law – is this monastic establishment Anglican or Roman Catholic? Or does it have close affinities with Orthodoxy? It is truly not easy to say, because it witnesses in a particular way to the need to bring together the debris of the one body.

## Catholic

It follows as a matter of course that the Church is to be described as holy, and we treat it with reverence. We also affirm in the creeds that it is catholic. This is frequently presented as equivalent to 'universal': the Church includes all Christians all over the world. Another key connotation of the word 'catholic', however, is 'mainstream'. The Church catholic, for all its variety, focuses around what can be identified as mainstream Christian belief, life and practice – and one of the tests is continuity through the ages. No manifestation of the Church is perfect, and there are degrees of catholicity, and through its history the monastic tradition has on the whole (there are always exceptions to everything, as we shall see) desired to situate itself within the optimum, to live as near as possible to what is the mainstream life of the Church. This notion of 'mainstream' refers to a continuity of life that can be called genetic, and so the creeds use 'apostolic' for this continuity, meaning passed on from the Apostles. You cannot treat the Bible like a flat-pack kit for setting up a church, without deriving it from the mainstream of Christian thought. Far from being a human machine with human engineers, the body of Christ passes on its life genetically from place to place and from generation to generation by passing on what it has received (the word 'tradition' means 'handing on'). If this might be thought a weak claim, we only need consider the English language to realize how it has all been passed on genetically – any language works on the equivalent to apostolic and catholic principles. In both a language and in the Church, everything has a derivation, which may go back hundreds or thousands of years, and the derivation can help us understand it.

## In Christ

These aspects of the Church enable it to engender a powerful sense of identity. For religious communities in particular, this is strong enough to be the source of a confidence that will never panic, however adverse the circumstances – this is significant in an age when many Christians are showing signs of panic. This confident identity is what St Paul means when he talks about being 'in Christ'. 'As many of you as were baptized into Christ have clothed yourselves with Christ. There is no longer Jew or Greek, there is no longer slave or free, there is no longer male and female; for all of you are one in Christ Jesus' (Gal. 3.27–28). For many members of the Corinthian church, their identity was still too much located in secular society and its ways. Paul berates them, for something much greater is theirs, the identity they find through being in Christ. 'Now you are the body of Christ and individually members of it' (1 Cor. 12.27). This identity is a corporate identity – we being many, are one body in Christ, and individually members one of another (Rom. 12.5). This body's roots are not secular society but 'in the air', coursing down from the divine mystery for which the Bible repeatedly uses images of up, sky, heaven (which are, of course, metaphorical). So in Colossians 3.3 Paul can say 'your life is hidden with Christ in God'.

## A business relationship, or one of love?

This being in Christ is not affected by bad behaviour. However badly its officers and members may behave, the body of Christ remains what it is, God's people 'in Christ' – Christ is there, waiting to be found in it. Confident love of the Church, particularly among those in religious communities, sits higher than the desire for the Church to succeed. This is crucial to understand – it is a key element in the countercultural nature of monasticism and, we must go on to say, in any church that is sufficiently in tune with the gospel. We all want success, but that desire is put in its place by the primary emphasis on relationships, not results. It would be difficult to love a church which is essentially a purely human organization. The Church, with its 'roots in the air', however, is a divine mystery that allows itself to be compromised on the surface by human sin and foolishness, but is greater and more effective than its sometimes-cracked surface. Beneath this surface it is holy, something that people are drawn to love because it is a face of God's love, the body of him who gave his life for us in love.

## Mental images

Abstract or invisible entities are always *imaged* by human beings. We automatically create an image in our minds. We have a mental image of Jesus or indeed of God, and we need to be reminded that our mental images will be inadequate. They are without exception limited images. If what we have been saying about the Church is the case, then the same applies: we have to take care about how we image it. Our images come from our experience. Renaissance artists painting the Nativity put the characters in Renaissance clothes; a midwife's image of Christ's birth, on the other hand, will reflect her daily experience as a midwife. In this light, to take the General Synod of the Church of England as an example, members could easily be led to feel this is like parliament, the governing body of a human organization: this is the decisive place where the future of the Church is to be determined. They could easily feel that this is the primary way in which the Church works its way forward. This is *it*. Such a view is probably not widespread, but a version of it affects all of us, as practical approaches to church business edge deeper aspects of the Church to the margins, something very evident in some reports and programmes.

Such a thing will be true of any denomination, in each case with a peculiar twist. This book aims to think ecumenically, and as Shepherds Law has had since its beginning a particular mission to span the Anglican and Roman Catholic churches, we will pay specific attention to these two churches. This will not be to the exclusion of others, but will take these two as working examples, acknowledging that their relationship is a significant one within the Christian family. Moving from the General Synod, then, we could imagine how attitudes might be with some people and bodies responsible for the Roman Catholic Church's governance and leadership as they deliberate and make decisions. Once again, there may be a sense that *this is it*. There is a problem here too, but a different one – a very real sense of the Church as a divine institution, but one which invests people in authority with power to exercise control. In the end such control is just as human-centred, but with greater reference to the divine mystery and to the tradition, seeing a need to defend them using straightforward legal methods accompanied by a willingness to coerce. Something has been lost, in relation to God's ability to do the unexpected, to be the one in charge. Thankfully not all, probably not most, Roman Catholic bodies and leaders fit this picture, but even among the most enlightened there is the dampening effect of the hand of control in this huge organization.

These problems do not just concern a *belief* about where the effectiveness lies – it is a matter of the *image* held before us, reflected in our minds and coursing in the bloodstream as a tacit but limited picture of the Church.

## Heavenly decision-making

Once again we have to say that such an approach cannot work in a monastery – it would be its undoing. The image of the Church with which religious communities find themselves working, sometimes even to their exasperation, is one that centres not on human decision-making, nor on fail-safe systems, but on grace. The tree is upside-down, its roots are above, not down here. This does not ignore the fact that the gospel is incarnational. Christ threw himself totally into human life, and we must do likewise. But we should greatly fear any treating of human life and the world in which we are set, or of solidified structures of belief, as an immovable resource and point of reference.

In the monastic tradition, this centring on grace affects everything, in ways that are tacit and intangible, but strongly guided by a quest – not for a meeting of minds, or a majority decision, or quick and effective action, or the following of preordained structures, even though there are times when those are particularly needed, but by a quest for the will of God, with preparedness to wait for the right moment for a sense of that to emerge. Decision-making is always closely related to worship, which is the decisive place where the Church's life and work are carried forward, and worship is loved with the same kind of tacit under-the-skin love that we find in any healthy family. Religious communities here are a signpost pointing to the invisible workings of God. A large part of their lives is a 'waste of time' – hours spent in prayer and quiet – and in contemplative communities, as much of the day as is practically possible is given over to this. It looks like a waste of lives. All the time, however, this prayer is feeding into God's hidden plumbing that runs throughout the world, contributing to God's purposes for the world. It is based on the belief that such prayer is efficacious and is elicited from us as a part of God's way of working with the universe. This is true furthermore of all Christian prayer and worship – prayer is serious work, contributing to the carrying forward of the gospel. Christ's body has many limbs and organs, and among them the religious communities make this their particular contribution. It is in this context that decision-making is pursued, without pushing and without panic.

## Living with a 'sense of the Church'

Just as human persons will always be tacitly aware of their family and all the other people with whom they belong – perhaps not in every case at the forefront of their minds, but always in their deeper unconscious – so the gospel calls us to the same kind of tacit awareness of the people of God, the Church. We are no longer just ourselves – we are in Christ; it is this that drives St Paul to remind his hearers repeatedly of who they now are. This tacit awareness can be particularly evident in perhaps four ways:

1 When we worship together, the worshipping group is not enclosed within itself if it is healthy, but neither can it rely entirely on the world, its wisdom, and its needs, for the quickening of its worship, always to be aware of the universal Church of which it is part, whose worship is a great ever-flowing stream in which the group is caught up at the times of worship.
2 When we pray individually, we are bound up with others: no Christian ever prays alone.

3  A Christian decision-making body should beware of operating at too human a level, but rather will be conscious of sitting under the mysterious, sovereign dimension of grace. The processes of discernment will involve more than merely human reasoning and debate, or reference to established certainties; the overriding awareness will be of the quest for the will of God, and the affinity of that quest with worship.

4  This tacit awareness will inhabit the whole bearing of every Christian. In baptism, our tacit awarenesses are at least in part transferred, so that our identity is no longer primarily in our family, but in Christ and the body of Christ into which baptism grafts us. So, for example, the present Archbishop of Canterbury could say publicly when it was shown that his father was not the one he thought, that it didn't loom large for him, because his identity was in Christ. We are enabled to live the Christian life to the full the more we are tacitly aware of our belonging.

This 'sense of the Church' should need no advocacy, for through most of Christian history it was effortlessly there. Two things in particular have worked to subvert it. One is the constant human tendency to shrink things back to the here-and-now and to the self: in this way, the Church has repeatedly regressed to behaviour that has been all too human. In the process, we come to concentrate on the Church as a *thing*, rather than on the core referent, who is Christ. This thing, this institution, we want to defend, and we want to make it suit what we think we need. And so it comes to be treated more and more as a human machine, while lip service may well be paid to its holiness. In the Western Church, such an approach is automatically associated with the later Middle Ages, where it might be thought the Church often failed to see the wood for the trees, as grace came to be seen as a commodity that could be gained through this-worldly transactions; but only a little thought is needed for us to realize that in all ages Christians have been constantly slipping into this, losing sight of the dimension of grace and falling back on merely human resources. In the medieval Church, however, there was a fundamental inconsistency: all of this human-centred living went on, while at the same time there was a powerful sense of being under God. There was indeed a 'sense of the Church', but it fitted ill with the way people often behaved, while all the time they held on to it with complete conviction, an inconsistent mindset which is difficult for us to enter into today. At some point, however, the sense of the Church began to recede into the background. Christians of a Catholic persuasion tend to associate it with the Reformation, but that is true only in a limited way. If we think of the Church of Luther or Calvin, or most Protestant streams that came to be established in Britain, there remained a powerful tacit awareness of being bound up with all the people of God in the life of prayer and godly living. The eucharistic rite in the Book of Common Prayer speaks of our being very members 'incorporate in the mystical body of thy son, which is the blessed company of all faithful people'. One Anglican example of this (not to mention the long Anglican tradition of popular participation in the daily offices[4]) is that of learning the collect for each Sunday and feast of the year, to be said daily in the family or private prayers. There were still old people who did this when I was a parish priest – a tradition strongly conscious of the Church and its worshipping life. Some aspects of this sense of the Church may have been weakened or lost after the Reformation, but it remained more real for Anglicans or Calvinists than it was for Roman Catholics.

The significant change came with the Enlightenment. At this point, people learnt to stand apart as observers of nature, and so the scientific method was born; they learnt to stand apart even from God and the Church and observe and assess them too, like fish on a slab. It was at this point, most markedly in the eighteenth century, that we began to stand apart from the dimension of grace. The Enlightenment is of course itself a gift from God, and has its part to play in human life – our problem is that for 200 years it was enthroned, placed at the summit. This is being eroded in many ways in modern times, as has been demonstrated in the writings of postmodern philosophers, but since reason was given a throne rather than the role of invaluable assistant, it subverted many Christians' inner sense of identity in the mystery of the Church. So it is possible sometimes to find a huge contrast between the approach to decision-making in a monastic chapter and in the approach in the Church at large.

In Anglican decision-making bodies the ground principles can sometimes appear to be the Enlightenment and practical planning, strategy rather grace. Some can be heard saying of a church report or discussion, 'but where is grace in all of this?' While in Anglicanism this approach to the well-being of the Church can think in terms of *management*, in the Roman Catholic Church the same takes more the form of *control* (we are always talking of strong tendencies in both churches, and should not discount many impressive people and bodies in both). Both of these ways of operating are usually well intentioned and supported by real conviction and prayerful lives, but lacking in essential elements of Christian discernment.

## Whose sense of the Church?

The tacit awareness of the Church of which we have been speaking comes in various forms. In the Reformation tradition today, which has been particularly affected by the Enlightenment, it can seem weak and incomplete. In the Roman Catholic Church, it is strong, but hampered by too quick an association with (and even confinement to) the structures of the Church, so that other Christian bodies fail to become a part of the Roman mental map. For many Roman Catholics, when they think of the Church, it will take an effort to include in their picture Anglicans for instance, or Methodists, the Evangelical churches, the Eastern Orthodox and the many small ancient churches of the East. The results of this can be a picture that is too enclosed, too institutional, short on the kind of idealism that can be found among many other Christians who long for unity. In addition, for many Roman Catholics there is a very focused understanding of authority and teaching. In a Synod for the Consecrated Life, a speaker suggested that a 'sense of being with the Church' (*sentire cum Ecclesia*) involves 'thinking with the Church, judging with the Church, having the criteria that the Church has'.[5] While this approach verges on a picture of the Church being in some way independent of believers (equating it so to speak with the hierarchy), it has something to say about mutual obedience in the body of Christ. For Anglicans, on the other hand, their sense of the Church tends to be less pyramidal than this and to require a sustained openness to something alive and shifting: a sense of the churches of all the traditions, caught up within the one great tradition, with a need to hold together messages and insights that are not always easy to hold together.

Among the Orthodox, on the other hand, a sense of the Church in the way we have been speaking of it is important, but comes less to the fore. There is a much stronger sense of the tradition and a powerful sense of the Church in heaven – less of the horizontal sense of the Church on earth. These are great generalizations, but in the space of this short chapter the distinctions need to be mentioned.

## Rome as source

There is a little more now to add about the Roman Catholic Church. A distinction needs to be made between jurisdiction and inheritance. The level of universal jurisdiction and authority officially claimed by the Roman Church does not find agreement among the other churches, who in varying ways look for some scaling down of such claims, even though they may recognize a primacy in the Bishop of Rome. This should not however skew our grasp of historical reality. For the Western Church at least, the core of our inheritance comes from the place where Peter and Paul chose to locate the crown of their ministry and sacrificed their lives. So, with a few exceptions, the Anglican Book of Common Prayer is a Roman book through and through, indebted ultimately to the worship that went on in Roman basilicas in the fourth and fifth centuries. Not only do Western liturgy and theology trace their roots to a Christianity that was from early on centred on Rome, but in modern times a great driving force for liturgical reform has been the thinking and practice of the Roman Catholic Church, and there is a similar indebtedness among contemporary religious communities in the churches of the Reformation. This fact of inheritance does not necessarily validate the jurisdictional claims, but we inherit it as a major component in our sense of who we are. If you like, Rome's jurisdictional claims are problematic, even to many who belong within it, and that should not be confused with the fact that the Roman inheritance is in our genes. In the world of religious communities of the churches of the Reformation, this can be perceived in different ways and degrees, but it should not be surprising to find that for some it looms large, for the religious life is very conscious of its genes. Such a recognition of inheritance amounts to an uncovering of deep layers within what is shared by all the churches. An obvious response to the diversity between and within the churches on a 'sense of the Church' is to say that they all need to be brought together. We have much to learn from each other to inform our mental picture, our tacit awareness, of the body of Christ, and in all of that the Church of Rome remains key.

## Air for believers' roots

This preamble on the Church has been necessary because monastic life cannot be understood without it. Religious communities are custodians today of things which rightly belong to all Christians, but are often only weakly grasped. Why, for many Christians, is this question of a sense of the Church now coming to the fore? One reason is that for at least some the parish is no longer providing all they are seeking. The level of commitment that people are prepared to give can often fail to be up to the task that lies before the parish. If a parish priest asks people to commit themselves a little more to something in parish life, one common picture is of everyone running for cover – it is more than we can manage. The people in our congregations on the whole are good people – we cannot lay the responsibility for the situation on them – it is more to do with the shepherding. Something is not right with the whole institution of the Church. In many parishes there is no longer a climate that can encourage people to move beyond the presuppositions and parameters of daily life in the world of today to a dimension that stands in contrast to it. And the few who are looking for more start to go elsewhere. The parish can have difficulty in enabling the 180° turn of the gospel, so that we would have strong roots 'in the air'. It can foster the moral life, give energy to the struggle for personal integrity and social justice, and it can for some, but not for many, foster the life of individual prayer. What it is short on is the capacity to root those things in their deepest source. Where this is the case, grace operates, as it were, at second remove, subordinated to something else: a Church that provides a supporting role for the human perceptions established in us by our society and using human ways of proceeding. Perhaps this is one reason why many are now flocking to monasteries and cathedrals, and throwing up the phenomenon of 'new monasticism', seeking horizons beyond what seems possible in many a parish.

Secondly, our lives are constantly mobile. Even if we are not frequently moving house, we are always on the move, always busy, always changing the context in which we are breathing. For this and other reasons we have become vulnerable to our individual 'take' on life. We even assume we have to have a 'take' on Jesus, if we are a Christian – what counts for me is my take on Jesus, with little sense that this needs to be stood on its head, not dependent on our perceiving of Christ, but on all the time being perceived lovingly and perceptively by him. Charles Williams, the writer and member of the Oxford company known as 'The Inklings', when once asked how he was, replied, 'in the city and under the mercy'. I often don't know what to make of God or of life, but that is not so important as the consciousness of being made something of by God.

## A Church that speaks to the imagination

We will be better able to change if we hear what the Church is. Christians today need to hear about the Church, not in terms of information, but through the ear of the heart. The whole of Scripture tells us that the heart is the key, that deep well at the centre of every human being which is the source of all that motivates and gives us energy. This hearing about the Church, therefore, needs to speak to our imaginations and our hearts, and this is what seems to happen for many people when they visit monasteries – they find themselves entering a climate which turns things on their heads, and in so doing brings us to an unexpected place, where we begin to perceive something new.

This book seeks to record something of the historic witness of the life of religious communities and to articulate it in an accessible way. It also seeks to address wider questions facing the whole of Christianity, while taking Shepherds Law as a 'worked example' of monastic life. Such a task needed to start with the Church, for on that stands everything else. The body of Christ is the source, the root, the core of energy from which everything flows. While monastic life is unlikely ever to cause a tremor on the Richter scale, that is only true in geophysical terms. Its concern is with the one who is bigger even than the Big Bang. The monastic phenomenon stands as a pointer to things overlooked, things to work wonders for our energy-levels.

After this introduction to our subject at the level of principle, the next several chapters give us stories, both ancient and recent, in all of which the thread of a 'sense of the Church' and the dimension of grace runs like a tacit underground stream.

## Notes

1 For example, Alasdair MacIntyre, *After Virtue*, London, Duckworth, 1981; David Bentley-Hart, *Atheist Delusions: The Christian Revolution and its Fashionable Enemies*, New Haven, CT and London, Yale University Press, 2009.

2 Quoted in C. Piccardo, *Living Wisdom: The Mission and Transmission of Monasticism*, Collegeville, MN, Liturgical Press, 2014, p. xxiv.

3 Hart, *Atheist Delusions*, pp. 121f. See also Nick Spencer, *The Evolution of the West: How Christianity has Shaped Our Values*, London, SPCK, 2016.

4 See George Guiver, *Company of Voices: Daily Prayer and the People of God*, Norwich, Canterbury Press, 2000, chapter 16.

5 Cardinal Angelo Sodano, speaking at the Synod for the Consecrated life, Rome, 1994.

# 2

# Northumbria's Long Tradition

## SARAH FOOT

The missionaries, who in the sixth and seventh centuries brought the Christian faith to the pagan Germanic peoples settled in the southern and eastern portions of the former Roman province of Britain, came from different parts of the Christian West, reflecting disparate ecclesial traditions. Yet they shared one characteristic that led the early English Church to develop on distinctive lines: an ideal of communal monastic living that encompassed both lay ministry and contemplation. Whether originating from Italy, Gaul or Ireland, the evangelists who preached the gospel to the Anglo-Saxons all went out to minister to their flock from communal monastic houses. They belonged to congregations of religious, gathered either around a bishop (as in the case of the Roman, Augustine of Canterbury, Frankish, Agilbert of Dorchester or the Irish, Aidan of Lindisfarne) or an abbot (such as Eata of Melrose and later Ripon, Cedd of Lastingham or Trumhere of Gilling). Described most articulately in the writings of the Venerable Bede, this mixed mode of life enabled those committed to a life in religion both to spend time in devotion and prayer, but also to share in the task of teaching the word to the lay population outside the walls of their monasteries. For some, however, the pressures and distractions of a coenobitic life into which the world so often intruded proved too great; these individuals sought to find opportunities for private contemplation at or just beyond the edges of monastic closures, or even by withdrawing entirely to live as anchorites. The creation of Shepherds Law hermitage on the top of a Northumberland hillside thus draws on a long tradition of the eremitical life in Northumbria, one that goes back to the earliest days of Christian worship among the English.

## British Christianity

As Bede knew well, the inhabitants of Britain, first brought within the bounds of the Roman Empire by Julius Caesar, had accepted the Christian faith from Pope Eleutherius in the time of a certain 'Lucius', a king in Britain in the middle years of the second century.[1] Describing the British as having 'preserved the faith they had received in peace and quiet' (until the time of Diocletian's persecution), Bede clearly saw the aboriginal dwellers in the island of *Britannia*, like the Romans, as a people of God. He distinguished them from the 'Saxons or Angles' (then still living in Germany, although harrying British shores with their raiding), whom he termed barbarians.[2] The British also 'attained to the great glory of bearing faithful witness to God',[3] in the person of the martyr, Alban, killed for his refusal to sacrifice to pagan gods. In Bede's day, Alban's shrine attracted renown because of the frequent miracles of healing performed there.[4] Although Bede seems not to have realized this, Pope Gregory the Great had respected the British of his own day as Christians, as he demonstrated in his commentary on Job (a work that pre-dates Augustine's mission to England). Gregory wrote, 'lo the tongue of Britain, which had known nothing but barbarous gnashing of teeth, has now long since begun to shout aloud the Hebrew Alleluia in divine praises'.[5] Initially, Bede gave a favourable account of the British Church, reporting how the Christian Britons managed to defeat their pagan enemies, with God fighting on their side, and so restored a widespread peace to the island after initial Saxon attacks.[6] The Britons' lapse into the Pelagian heresy (the denying of original sin and refusal to accept the need for grace) brought the Gaulish bishop, Germanus, to Britain to restore orthodox belief. But that achieved and the teachers of the heresy banished, Bede could argue that 'the faith remained untainted in those parts for a very long time'.[7] As long as some among the population still remembered the calamity and bloodshed of the previous foreign wars, their behaviour remained 'within bounds'. However, Bede reported (here closely following his source, Gildas, *On the Ruin of Britain*), when those people died, 'a generation succeeded which knew nothing of all these troubles and was used only to the present state of peace'. Falling from the right path, the population descended into untruth and injustice, adding to other 'unspeakable crimes', the fact that 'they never preached the faith to the Saxons or Angles who inhabited Britain with them'.[8]

From this point of his *History* onwards, Bede's attitude to the British changed markedly. As a direct consequence of their failure to evangelize their new pagan neighbours, Bede argued, the British had forfeited God's favour and had become the 'unchosen race', the other against whom the English constructed their own Christian identity.[9] His antipathy did not rest only on earlier generations, but encompassed Bede's own contemporaries. This people had, he believed, so consistently and obdurately rejected the Roman Church's teachings about the correct calculation of Easter and the nature of the tonsure that he could argue 'to this very day it is the habit of the Britons to despise the faith and religion of the English and not to communicate with them in anything more than with the heathen';[10] elsewhere Bede observed that the Britons 'still persist in their errors and stumble in their ways'.[11] Having so determinedly cast the British in this light (perhaps because he saw their persistence in holding to the wrong Easter as a continuing denial of grace),[12] Bede played down the extent to which the British Church in fact continued to thrive in the southwest, western and northern parts of Britain, building on the rich heritage it had inherited from the Roman past, of which some material remains survive.[13] Continuities of church life, ecclesiastical organization and land-holding are most marked in the west midlands (for example at Gloucester, Worcester and Lichfield) and in the south-west (at Sherborne or Wareham), but may have extended to other places as well.[14] Stephen, biographer of Bishop Wilfrid, wrote tantalizingly about a list of the consecrated places in various parts, which the British clergy had deserted when fleeing from the hostile sword wielded by Northumbrian warriors, lands that Wilfrid had come to hold for the service of God, but we know no more about the location of these, or of what they might have consisted.[15] The one British cleric whose evangelizing work Bede did praise – Ninian, who preached to the southern Picts and established a church at Whithorn in Galloway (*Candida Casa*) that later came under Northumbrian rule – stood out from most of his compatriots because he had studied in Rome, where he would have learnt about the Catholic Easter and other Roman customs.[16] Bede said little about British monasticism (beyond noting the importance of their most famous monastery, Bangor Iscoed), but he did make reference to one Briton who apparently lived as an anchorite, although he did not name him. This 'holy and prudent man' was consulted by the British bishops before they met with Bishop Augustine of Canterbury for the second time to discuss whether they would participate in his mission to the English. The hermit's recommendation that they should ignore Augustine's teachings if he failed in humility to stand at the arrival of the British delegation played no small part in the descent of that meeting into acrimony.[17]

## The Conversion of Northumbria

Two distinct groups of missionaries worked to teach the faith to the pagan inhabitants of Northumbria: first a Roman mission, led by Paulinus, who accompanied Aethelburh, the daughter of Aethelberht, first Christian king of Kent, when she married the still-pagan Edwin in 619.[18] Although a visionary experience encouraged Edwin personally to accept Christianity, he had to persuade his followers to come with him to baptism.[19] Bede thus provided one of the most vivid and memorable passages of his *History*, creating a narrative of a meeting of the king's council at which various figures spoke in support of the new faith. An unnamed nobleman showed his understanding of the Church's promises of salvation by likening the life of man on earth to the journey of a sparrow through the king's hall, while the pagan 'high priest', Coifi, announced his recognition of the worthlessness of the religion he had professed and symbolically profaned his own shrine, destroying its idols.[20] Paulinus became Bishop of York in 625 and baptized the king and his followers in a hastily constructed wooden church at York on Easter Day in 627 (on which occasion Hild, the future abbess of Whitby and a great-niece of the king, was also initiated into the faith).[21] Here we see employed the same missionary methods as used previously in Kent (and in Essex and East Anglia), by which the evangelists began at the top of the social scale, converting the king and his court, before reaching out to a wider population.[22]

Like the members of the first Roman mission to Kent, the clergy who accompanied Paulinus brought from Rome a knowledge of

Pope Gregory the Great's teachings about how to integrate pastoral involvement with the laity (and specifically the work of mission and evangelization) into the contemplative life, from which, of course, the call of the external world would seem to distract. Having had to confront these tensions in his own life, Gregory was well equipped to offer advice, recognizing how much the work of the pastor would always necessitate the surrendering of quiet contemplation: 'By contemplation we rise to the love of God; by preaching we return to the service of our neighbour', he wrote in his commentary on Job.[23] As Robert Markus has argued, for Gregory 'contemplation had to be considered in the context of the pastor's function in the Christian community, and, conversely, the pastoral ministry itself had a radically contemplative direction'.[24] That understanding goes a long way to resolving the apparent paradox of sending monks to take the word to the pagan English at the ends of the earth, but as we shall see, many monk-pastors struggled to find sufficient space to fulfil all their personal spiritual needs (and so achieve through private contemplation the necessary preparation to enable them to preach effectively to their flock).

Although initially successful, the first Northumbrian mission was abruptly halted by the death of King Edwin at the hands of the pagan kings Cadwallon of Gwynedd and Penda of Mercia in 633. The ensuing political chaos in Northumbria forced Paulinus to flee back to Kent with Aethelburh, her daughter Eanflaed and two small sons. Only James the Deacon ('a true churchman and a saintly man') remained in Northumbria to carry on the work of teaching and baptizing from a village near Catterick, which bore his name; renowned as a church musician, James lived long enough to participate in the Synod of Whitby in 664.[25] Meanwhile, Northumbria lapsed back into paganism as the kingdom's rulers, the sons of Aethelfrith, gave up their adherence to Christianity.[26]

This period of Northumbrian history proved so unfortunate that Bede reported 'those who compute the dates of kings' elected to abolish the memory of those perfidious kings and instead attribute the year to their successor, King Oswald, one of the great heroes of Bede's *History*.[27] Having converted to Christianity while in exile with the Irish on Iona, Oswald invited the monks from that island community to send a mission to evangelize his people. After a first unsuccessful attempt by a man 'of harsh disposition', whose preaching the Northumbrians rejected, the monks sent Aidan (Bede's Anglicization of the Irish name, Áedán), who recommended the introduction of God's word, in Aidan's paraphrase, 'with the milk of simpler teaching' (1 Cor. 3.2), thus demonstrating his own discretion, 'the mother of virtues'.[28] Aidan stands out in the pages of Bede's History as one of those whose example he most commended to his readers from the moment of his first introduction. Thus he described the bishop as 'a man of outstanding gentleness, devotion and moderation, who had a zeal for God', although – and here Bede's scrupulousness caused him to qualify his praise – he did not practise his zeal 'entirely according to knowledge', referring in this respect to Aidan's following of the Irish method for calculating Easter and the Irish tonsure. He praised the Irishman for using the king (who had fluent Irish) to interpret the heavenly word for his leading men, until such time as Aidan became more practised in the English language.[29] Aidan established an episcopal seat at Lindisfarne and gathered there a group of monks around him. This arrangement whereby the bishop's clergy were also monks and subject to the abbot within the monastery would have appeared less unusual in Ireland than it did to those accustomed to Roman habits. Bede compared Aidan's congregation favourably with that first established at Canterbury under Augustine, likening both to the first community established by the Apostles in Jerusalem and described in the Acts of the Apostles. Having no possessions of their own but sharing all in common, these holy men sought to live the life of the gospel that they preached.[30]

## Monk-bishops and priests

To Bede, Aidan's virtues did not rest solely on the performance of missionary activities or his creation of the bishopric at Lindisfarne, even though he and the congregation gathered round him represented an ideal model of pastors and teachers, bringing the faith as well as to the nobility in the king's immediate circle to the Northumbrian peasantry, who dwelt in scattered upland settlements.[31] Aidan stood out as the first of the monk-bishops for whom Bede showed particular admiration, exemplifying the monastic way of life through the exercise of his episcopal ministry and through his personal asceticism and devotion.[32] As Bede explained, 'Aidan taught the clergy many lessons about the conduct of their lives, but above all he left them a most salutary example of abstinence and self-control; and the best recommendation of his teaching to all was that he taught them no other way of life than that which he himself practised among his fellows'.[33] He took no interest in worldly possessions, preferring to give away such gifts as he had received to those more needy than himself as alms, and rejecting the trappings of a noble lifestyle; once he even gave the king's gift of a horse away to a beggar.[34] Aidan's preference for travelling on foot gave him the opportunity more easily to approach a rural lay population and invite them either to learn about the mysteries of the faith or to have their existing understanding reinforced.[35]

Aidan's life and ministry bore witness to the tensions already mentioned that affected those who aspired to maintain the ideals of monastic contemplation, while willingly assuming the burdens of episcopal office, pressures that were not of course unique to English circumstances.[36] The necessity to sustain close relations with ruling kings both to ensure their continuing commitment to the faith and also to encourage the members of ruling families and their leading nobles to make gifts to the Church, inevitably took bishops away from their ecclesiastical companions, requiring them to spend time in the company of noble warriors and their wider retinues. While meetings of the king's council and royal feasts might well have provided opportunities for hortatory instruction of individuals and groups, they also necessarily disrupted bishops' own spiritual lives and those of the clergy who accompanied them. According to Bede, Aidan laid great stress on the importance of the daily reading of the Scriptures and memorizing the Psalms. He used to take his companions away from feasts and other gatherings of the laity, in order that they might spend time together in reading or in prayer. To the bishop, this provided one means of compensating for his forced separation from the discipline of life in community, yet his behaviour had an impact on others beyond his immediate entourage. For, Bede reported, a number of men and women instructed by his example began to make it their habit to fast regularly on Wednesdays and Fridays, except in the season between Easter and Pentecost.[37] On other occasions, when not required at the king's side, Aidan withdrew even from the rest of the monks at Lindisfarne, retreating to the island of Farne (less than two miles away from the royal city of Bamburgh) in order to pray in solitude and silence; Bede had seen the site of his solitary habitation which remained on the island in his own day.[38]

Other monk-bishops sought likewise to distance themselves from the world when they could. Cedd, bishop of the East Saxons, accepted a gift from Ethelwald, the son of King Oswald who ruled over Deira, choosing a site for a monastery amid steep and remote hills at Lastingham in North Yorkshire. He spent the whole season of Lent in this place, making it fit for consecration through his prayer and fasting. Although Cedd's duties in Essex took him away from his monastery, he returned as often as he could, electing unfortunately to do so in 664 during an outbreak of plague at the monastery from which he died.[39] Archbishop Theodore brought Cedd's brother Chad, out of retirement at Lastingham (where he served as abbot after his brother's death) to become bishop of the Mercians and people of Lindsey. He, too, built himself a more retired dwelling place not far from his own episcopal seat at Lichfield, where he could read and pray privately with seven or eight of his fellow monks; he happened to be on retreat there with just one monk when the time came for him, too, to die.[40] Similarly, when John of Beverley became Bishop of Hexham, he made use of an oratory in a remote dwelling, enclosed by a rampart amid some trees, about a mile and a half from Hexham, across the River Tyne. John used to take small groups of companions with him to spend time in prayer and reading when occasion allowed, making a particular habit of retreating there during Lent. Even while thus removed from the bustle of the world, John still continued to look after his flock, making sure during one Lent that he took care of a local young man, curing him of an unsightly skin disease and teaching him to speak.[41] In John's case at least, personal devotion had to take second place to episcopal duty, and those of his immediate circle who accompanied him on retreat also still had some interaction with the local lay population.

In these examples of monk-bishops with eremitical leanings, we see how the two strands of ecclesial tradition that had worked for the Christianization of Northumbria had found fusion in the north of England in the generations after the conversion period, particularly after the Synod of Whitby in 664 had resolved the differences between those with Irish and Roman backgrounds over the correct calculation of the date of Easter. King Oswiu's decision to ally himself to St Peter and the Roman party ensured that the Northumbrian Church harnessed itself to the mainstream of Western European Christianity.[42] Writing to the king after the synod to congratulate him on its outcome, Pope Vitalian quoted a series of Old Testament prophecies that he believed fulfilled in Oswiu's day, enabling him to argue: 'Most excellent son, as you see, it is clearer than day that it is here foretold that not only you but also all peoples will believe in Christ, the Maker of all things.'[43] Some of the defeated Irish party, including the Bishop of Lindisfarne Colman, returned to Ireland after the synod, unwilling to accept either the Roman Easter, or that Church's style of tonsure.[44] But others, including the brothers Cedd and Chad, although brought up in the Ionan tradition, agreed to adopt the Roman customs. The travelling missionary style of evangelization practised by those of Irish background and the somewhat less mobile Roman customs, which saw clergy working out of fixed monastic bases, now existed side by side in the Northumbrian Church, as all united in the work of ministering to a still imperfectly Christianized population.

Priests lay at the heart of the Church's pastoral ministry. Bishops remained few in number and, as Bede's hortatory letter to his own diocesan in 734 suggested, they frequently struggled to reach all areas of their vast dioceses, leaving priests with the regular work of providing for the laity.[45] Some of those priests belonged to episcopal households and travelled with their bishop wherever he travelled, probably sharing in some of the work of preaching. Others, however, came from monasteries, for as we have already seen, all ecclesiastics (priests, lesser clergy, monks and nuns) lived in community.[46] Bede laid considerable stress on the obligations of ordained clergy to minister the sacraments to the laity; in a sermon for Epiphany (on the baptism of Christ) he urged 'let as many of us as have been advanced to priestly rank humbly fulfil the office imposed upon us of dispensing his sacraments'.[47] On another occasion, preaching about St Peter, Bede reminded his audience that just as Christ gave the Holy Spirit to his Disciples and granted them the power to determine whether the sins of the people should be forgiven or not, 'even so the same office is committed to the whole Church in her bishops and priests, so that when she has come to know sinners' cases, she considers which are humble and truly penitent, and in compassion she may absolve them', whereas she may suggest that 'those who persist in sins that they have committed, should be consigned to eternal punishment'.[48] In addition to exercising these specifically sacerdotal functions, priests also had a duty to preach, to exhort the faithful and to convert those who remained in the ignorance of heathenism; the role of preaching could extend beyond the ranks of the ordained to encompass others (probably even women), but it fell particularly on the priesthood.[49] The same emphasis on the sacramental role of priests appears in the Penitential attributed to Archbishop Theodore (archbishop from 669 to 690), and in the canons of eighth-century church councils, especially that of *Clofesho* in 747, which mentioned specifically the places and regions of the laity assigned to priests for their particular cure.[50] These tasks remained as compelling for the generations who ministered in Northumbria after Whitby as they had been for the first generations of evangelists. Yet, inevitably, such obligations conflicted with the contemplative aspirations of monks and priests alike, causing some to look for means by which to withdraw at least occasionally from the world in solitude (or with only a few, carefully chosen companions).

## The search for solitude

Among those whom Bede singled out for particular praise in the pages of his *History*, men who contrived to combine an active pastoral ministry with an ascetic spirituality stand out above all, notably the bishops whom we have already discussed. Yet others as well as bishops felt the need for separation from external distraction and sought out spaces appropriate to fulfil that desire.[51] Fursa had preached for a long time in Ireland before, tired of the noise of the crowds who thronged to hear his teaching, he left his native island to travel with a few companions into the kingdom of the East Angles, where he preached and founded a monastery. Still determined to live as a hermit, he and his brother managed to survive for a year by the labour of their own hands until fear of heathen invasion drove them from the kingdom to find refuge in Gaul, where Fursa died.[52] That pattern of alternating pastoral work with withdrawn contemplation characterized Cuthbert also. According to his anonymous first biographer he lived as a monk at Lindisfarne 'following the contemplative amid the active life',[53] but still desired to obtain more solitude. At the first beginning of his solitary life, Bede reported, Cuthbert retired to a place in the outer precincts of the monastery which seemed more secluded; but when he had fought there alone for some time by prayer and fasting, he looked for a yet more remote place of combat.[54] He elected to build himself a hermitage on the island of Farne (once having driven out the resident demons), in order to retire alone (except on those occasions when he needed others of the monks to help him in manual tasks beyond his own capacity).[55] Cuthbert's biographer portrayed the manner of Cuthbert's solitary life in language that closely echoed the Life of St Antony, just as many of his miracles imitated those attributed to St Martin, showing how the Northumbrian saint's eremitic practices placed him in a long and distinguished tradition of holy men.[56] When he (reluctantly) became Bishop of Lindisfarne, Cuthbert had to leave Farne and found himself travelling widely across his diocese to minister to all his flock.[57] In his last illness, however, he resigned the 'worldly honours' of the bishopric and returned to his island retreat to die.[58] Bede's reworking of the earlier life (once in verse and then again in a prose life, plus some chapters recounting further miracles that he added to the end of the fourth book of the *History*) presented the saint as an exemplary pastor and teacher, who never swerved from his devotion to the ideal of contemplation; his image of Cuthbert owed a good deal to Gregorian models, especially Gregory's depiction of St Benedict in his Dialogues.[59]

Both the anonymous biographers and Bede stressed the fact that Cuthbert's experience of life in community had prepared him for the more arduous life of a hermit, one that was not to be entered into lightly. Others similarly came to the solitary life only after a period of preparation in monastic living. Thus Ultán, the brother of Fursa, spent 'a long time of probation in the cloister', before he joined his brother as a hermit;[60] and Guthlac had trained for two years in the monastery at Repton, where he developed an interest in the desert fathers, only eventually obtaining permission to adopt the eremitical life himself, in the 'dismal fen of immense size' at Crowland.[61] On this remote island haunted

by demons, Guthlac lived as an anchorite for the last 15 years of
his life; the account that Felix constructed of his spiritual battles
and heroic asceticism drew closely on the examples presented
by both St Antony and St Cuthbert.[62] When making arrange-
ments for his own death, Guthlac spoke about his sister, Pega,
'holy virgin of Christ' and 'handmaiden of God', who reputedly
lived as an anchoress at Peakirk (near Crowland), and another
anchorite called Ecgberht, whom the saint was confident would
have divine knowledge of his fate.[63] Ecgberht had provided the
cloth in which the saint's body was originally buried, in which
Pega rewrapped it after she had discovered her brother's body
to be incorrupt, a year after his death.[64] Another member of
the Repton community, Caelin, who served as *praepositus*, had
previously been a solitary and held office in Wilfrid's minster
for a long time before the bishop finally gave him permission
to return to his former way of life.[65] Cynefrith, the brother of
Abbot Coelfrith of Jarrow, served for many years as Abbot of
Gilling (where his brother first took monastic vows), but gave
up the abbacy to withdraw to Ireland in order to spend more
time learning the Scriptures and serving the Lord with tears and
prayers, presumably in solitude.[66] Bede mentioned other Anglo-
Saxon religious who went to Ireland in search of the eremitical
life, including Wihtberht, later a missionary among the Frisians,
who had formerly lived for many years as a hermit in Ireland, 'in
great perfection of life'.[67]

Also a certain Haemgils, an eminent priest, who had lived in
the vicinity of Dryhthelm's cell at Melrose and heard from him
his vision of the other world; in Bede's day this holy man lived
in solitude in Ireland, 'supporting his declining years on a scanty
supply of bread and cold water'.[68] Others travelled farther afield:
a man called Philip, *genere Angulus*, who had spent time in Rome,
lived as a hermit near the river Pfrimm in the Rhineland in the
eighth century, while a certain Sola became a hermit in the diocese of Willibald, of whom the village of Solnhofen near Eichstätt
preserved memory.[69] Two English sisters lived as hermits at
Oberalteich in ninth-century Bavaria.[70]

Nearer to home, an anchorite, Ethelwald, succeeded Cuthbert
in the solitary life on Farne Island; he had for many years previously served as a priest in the monastery at Ripon and went

on to spend 12 years on Farne before he died. He was buried in the church on the island of Lindisfarne.[71] Ethelwald in turn was succeeded by a certain Felgild, whose face was cured of a disfiguring redness and swelling by the relics of St Cuthbert.[72] We know of another anchorite, Billfrith, who probably lived close to Lindisfarne in the second half of the eighth century. According to the Old English colophon added by the scribe Aldred to the Lindisfarne Gospels while they were at Chester-Le-Street in the tenth century: 'Billfrith, the anchorite, forged the ornaments which are on the outside, and adorned it with gold and gems and gilt-silver, pure metal.'[73] Headed by Ethelwald (Oedilwald), these three Lindisfarne hermits were included in the list of the 28 anchorites (all of them priests), whose names were recorded in the early ninth-century Durham *Liber Vitae*.[74] Other figures named in the same list who can now be identified are Hereberct, a hermit on Derwent Water and friend of Cuthbert's (see further below); Wihtberht, the companion of Ecgberht in Ireland; Haemgils, the priest from near Melrose; a certain Balthere, hermit at Tyningham, whose death was recorded in 756 in the first set of Northern Annals preserved by Simeon of Durham in his *Historia Regum*;[75] Echha, who died in 767 and had been a hermit at Crayke in North Yorkshire;[76] and Cuthred, a priest of Lindisfarne *c*.793.[77] The list also included the name of Boisil, whom we might want to identify with the prior of Melrose when Cuthbert first joined that community, but no other source reported that he had ever lived as a hermit, and this might be another man of the same name.[78] The *Liber Vitae* did not, however, name another anchorite, Alchfrith, who lived near Lindisfarne *c*.780 and wrote three prayers now preserved in the Book of Cerne, plus a letter (or sermon) addressed to Hyglac, lector and priest.[79]

Alcuin (the deacon from the cathedral church of York who worked as a scholar in the court of Charlemagne) mentioned several of these hermits in his poem on the bishops, kings and saints of York. He praised Wihtberht, who led a life of contemplation in strict solitude;[80] Balthere as a mighty warrior, who waged war against the spirits of the air while living on Bass Rock in the Firth of Forth;[81] Echa, who lived a life of chastity, shunning worldly honours in order to enjoy heavenly ones in future; 'by leading the life of an angel devoutly on earth, he predicted much of the future like a prophet'.[82] It would appear that the various monastic communities associated with Bishop Wilfrid had connections with several anchorites, for when news of the imminence of the bishop's death spread, 'all his abbots and anchorites came hastening from their homes by day and by night' in order to reach him while he still lived.[83] We know nothing else about the identity of these individuals, however.

True hermits – men (or women) who lived entirely solitary lives, cut off from all interaction with the world around them – do not appear in the sources from this period, perhaps for the obvious reason that (had any such contrived to sustain a genuinely isolated life) no one knew enough of their feats of spiritual heroism to recount them to future generations.[84] Some tried to adopt the eremitical life but found themselves (like St Antony before them) forced to provide spiritual succour to those who came to their doors, attracted by reports of their exemplary behaviour and performance of miracles. One such, a certain Wilgils, who tried to live as a hermit on Spurn Head, ended up with a religious community gathered round him, supported by grants of estates on the headland made by the king and his leading nobles.[85] Guthlac also had frequent lay and ecclesiastical visitors to his watery hermitage in the fens at Crowland, including Headda, Bishop of Lichfield, and Aethelbald, future king of the Mercians.[86] After Guthlac's death another hermit, Cissa (a priest), lived in his cell and received gifts from King Aethelbald.[87] Although neither Bede nor Cuthbert's anonymous hagiographer provided any information about the background of the priest Hereberct who lived as a hermit on an island in Derwent Water, we may assume from the fact of his ordination that he had formerly belonged to a religious community of some sort. Hereberct used frequently to seek out Cuthbert's company in order to listen to his teaching and engage in spiritual conversation, and enjoyed the privilege of dying at the same moment as the saint, to be received with him into the heavenly bliss.[88]

Not all who sought out the eremitical life earned the respect of their contemporaries. Guthlac's biographer, Felix, reported that one man in the saint's retinue, Wigfrith, had previously lived among the Irish (Scotti), where he had encountered false hermits and pretenders of various religions whom he found able to predict the future and perform other miracles, though he knew not by what power; he believed he could confidently distinguish such charlatans from the followers of true religion.[89]

## Prayer in the world

Few of those called to a life in religion in the first Christian centuries in Northumbria seem ever to have achieved a complete separation between their cloistered existence and the world outside its walls, and we may doubt that many genuinely aspired so to do. Although the model of the desert saint proved attractive to many early English monks (and a few nuns) particularly, it would seem, in Northumbria (where the majority of those of whom record has survived appear to have lived), the model of the solitary ascetic did not meet with unqualified approval in all quarters of the contemporary Church. As we have already seen, Bede argued articulately for the direct involvement of the members of monastic communities, especially those in priestly orders, in preaching, teaching and administering the sacraments to their lay neighbours. Priests were central to Bede's vision of a teaching pastorate, and he placed heavy burdens on them, expecting them not to marry and to live ascetic and devoted lives.[90] Just as priests needed to spend time in withdrawn contemplation, monks came closer to perfection only after lives of virtuous action.[91] Occasional withdrawal to a place of solitude for more intense contemplation, Bede commended; but complete separation into desert wildernesses could not serve the needs of a (literally) mission-shaped Church. Even Cuthbert, whose asceticism attracted Bede's warmest praise, remained firmly rooted in the active life. As Thacker has argued, Bede portrayed the saint's solitude as the crowning accomplishment of the monk: 'from the long *perfectio* of the active life, Cuthbert rose to the ultimate *otium* of divine contemplation'.[92] Cuthbert himself approved and commended the coenobitic life as a sufficient route to holiness. Addressing his own community Cuthbert said, 'But the life of monks ought rightly to be admired, for they are in all things subject to the commands of the abbot and govern all their times of watching, prayer, fasting and working by his judgement.'[93]

Despite the manifest interest in ascetic separation felt by many in the seventh- and eighth-century Church, the needs of the pastoral requirements of the Church came to prevail over individual spiritual aspirations. The example of those holy monk-bishops whose lives Bede so commended demonstrates most clearly how the manifest tensions between the ideal of personal devotion and the necessity to meet the wider needs of the laity might best be reconciled. The obligation of priests and bishops to follow Christ the good shepherd and tend to the needs of the flock ultimately had to prevail. In a sermon on Christ's Nativity, Bede interpreted the shepherds to whom the angel brought the news of the infant's birth at Bethlehem mystically to symbolize the teachers of flocks and directors of souls of the faithful; for 'the time was drawing near when the supremely good Shepherd would, by shepherds sent into the world, recall to the always-green pastures of heavenly life his sheep who were wandering, scattered far and wide'.[94] Brother Harold now lives at Shepherds Law as heir to this long Northumbrian tradition of a mixed life of prayerful contemplation and action.

## Notes

1 Bede, *Historia Ecclesiastica*, I.14, ed. and trans. Bertram Colgrave and R. A. B. Mynors, *Bede's Ecclesiastical History of the English People*, Oxford, Oxford University Press, 1969, pp. 24–5 [hereafter *HE*].

2 W. Trent Foley and Nicholas J. Higham, 'Bede on the Britons', *Early Medieval Europe* 17 (2009), pp. 154–85 (at 157).

3 Bede, *HE*, I.6, pp. 28–9.

4 Bede, *HE*, I.7, pp. 28–35.

5 Gregory, *Moralia in Iob*, XXVII.xi.21, quoted by Clare Stancliffe, 'The British Church and the Mission of Augustine', in Richard Gameson (ed.), *St Augustine and the Conversion of England*, Stroud, Sutton, 1999, pp. 111–12.

6 Bede, *HE*, I.20, pp. 62–5.

7 Bede, *HE*, I.21, pp. 64–7. See Rowan Williams, 'Theology and the Paschal Controversy: Bede's Case Against the British Church', in Santha Bhattacharji, Dominic Mattos and Rowan Williams (eds), *Prayer and Thought in Monastic Tradition: Essays in Honour of Benedicta Ward SLG*, London, T&T Clark, 2014, pp. 31–44.

8 Bede, *HE*, I.22, pp. 68–9. For Gildas, see M. Winterbottom (ed.), *The Ruin of Britain, and Other Works*, London, Phillimore & Co., 1978, and M. Lapidge and D. N. Dumville (eds), *Gildas: New Approaches*, Woodbridge, Boydell, 1984.

9 Alexander Murray, 'Bede and the Unchosen Race', in Huw Pryce and John Watts (eds), *Power and Identity in the Middle Ages: Essays in Memory of Rees Davies*, Oxford, Oxford University Press, 2007, pp. 52–67.

10 Bede, *HE*, II.20, pp. 204–5.

11 Bede, *HE*, V.22, pp. 554–5.

12 Williams, 'Theology and the Paschal Controversy', pp. 41–4.

13 Malcolm Lambert, *Christians and Pagans: The Conversion of Britain from Alban to Bede*, New Haven, CT and London, Yale University Press, 2010, pp. 1–43.

14 Steven Bassett, 'Church and Diocese in the West Midlands: The Transition from British to Anglo-Saxon Control', in J. Blair and R. Sharpe (eds), *Pastoral Care Before the Parish*, Leicester, Leicester University Press, 1992, pp. 13–40; cf. Patrick Sims-Williams, *Religion and Literature in Western England 600–800*, Cambridge, Cambridge University Press, 1990, pp. 54–86.

15 Stephen, *Vita S. Wilfridi*, ch. 17, ed. and trans. Bertram Colgrave, *The Life of Bishop Wilfrid by Eddius Stephanus*, Cambridge, Cambridge University Press, 1927, pp. 36–7.

16 Bede, *HE*, III.4, pp. 222–3.

17 Bede, *HE*, II.2, pp. 138–9.

18 Bede, *HE*, II.9, pp. 162–7; Henry Mayr-Harting, *The Coming of Christianity to Anglo-Saxon England*, 3rd edn, London, Pennsylvania State University Press, 1991, pp. 66–7.

19 Bede, *HE*, II.12, pp. 176–81.

20 Bede, *HE*, II.13, pp. 182–7; cf. Julia Barrow, 'How Coifi pierced Christ's Side: A Re-examination of Bede's *Ecclesiastical History* II, Chapter 13', *Journal of Ecclesiastical History* 62 (2011), pp. 693–706.

21 Bede, *HE*, II.14, pp. 186–7.

22 For discussion of the ways in which missionaries taught the basics of Christian belief, see Carolyn Twomey, 'Kings as Catechumens: Royal Conversion Narratives and Easter in Bede's Historia Ecclesiastica', *Haskins Society Journal* 25 (2014), pp. 1–18.

23 Gregory, *Moralia in Iob*, VI.37.59; quoted by Robert Markus, *Gregory the Great and his World*, Cambridge, Cambridge University Press, 1997, p. 23.

24 Markus, *Gregory*, p. 26; see also Alan Thacker, 'Bede's Ideal of Reform', in Patrick Wormald, Donald Bullough and Roger Collins (eds), *Ideal and Reality in Frankish and Anglo-Saxon Society*, Oxford, Basil Blackwell, 1983, pp. 130–53 (at 142–4).

25 Bede, *HE*, II.20, pp. 206–7; III.25, pp. 298–9. The name of the village where James lived is now unknown, but it was identified as 'seynt Iemestret' in a fifteenth-century manuscript of the *History*, perhaps on the basis of that scribe's local knowledge: C. Plummer, *Venerabilis Baedae opera historica*, 2 vols, Oxford, Oxford University Press, 1896, II.118.

26 Bede, *HE*, III.1, pp. 212–13; on the apostasy of kings' sons, see Barbara Yorke, 'The Adaptation of the Anglo-Saxon Royal Courts to Christianity', in Martin Carver (ed.), *The Cross Goes North: Processes of*

*Conversion in Northern Europe 300–1300*, Woodbridge, Boydell, 2003, pp. 243–57 (at 244–5).

27 Bede, *HE*, III.1, pp. 214–15; for discussion of the 'gallery of good examples' found in Bede's pages, see James Campbell, *Essays in Anglo-Saxon History*, London, Hambledon Press, 1986, pp. 1–27.

28 Bede, *HE*, III.5, pp. 228–9.

29 Bede, *HE*, III.3, pp. 218–21; cf. Benedicta Ward, *The Venerable Bede*, London, Geoffrey Chapman, 1990 (reprinted 1998), p. 38.

30 Bede, *HE*, IV.27, pp. 434–5; cf. Bede, *Vita S Cuthberti*, ch. 16, ed. and trans. Bertram Colgrave, *Two Lives of Saint Cuthbert*, Cambridge, Cambridge University Press, 1940, pp. 142–307 (at pp. 208–9); Thacker, 'Bede's Ideal of Reform', p. 144.

31 Bede, *HE*, III.26, pp. 308–11.

32 Alan Thacker, 'Monks, Preaching and Pastoral Care in Early Anglo-Saxon England', in John Blair and Richard Sharpe (eds), *Pastoral Care Before the Parish*, Leicester, Leicester University Press, 1992, pp. 137–70 (at 153).

33 Bede, *HE*, III.5, pp. 226–7.

34 Bede, *HE*, III.14, pp. 258–9.

35 Bede, *HE*, III.5, pp. 226–7.

36 Compare, for example, the case of St Martin of Tours, who created for himself a cell near his cathedral church where he hoped to pray uninterrupted, but who also sometimes found it necessary to repair to a hermitage a short distance away at Marmoutier in order to escape unwanted visitors: Sulpicius Severus, *Vita S Martini*, ed. J. Fontaine, Sources Chrétiennes 133, Paris, Éditions du Cerf, 1967, chs 6–7, 10, pp. 264–9, 272–5; Clare Stancliffe, *Saint Martin and his Hagiographer*, Oxford, Clarendon Press, 1983, pp. 149–53.

37 Bede, *HE*, III.5, pp. 226–7.

38 Bede, *HE*, III.16, pp. 262–3.

39 Bede, *HE*, III.23, pp. 286–9.

40 Bede, *HE*, IV.3, pp. 336–47. D. H. Farmer, 'Ceadda (*d*. 672?)', *Oxford Dictionary of National Biography*, Oxford, Oxford University Press, 2004. The late ninth-century *Old English Martyrology* recorded Chad's virtues and reported that another hermit St Ecgberht (*sancte Ecgberht se ancra*) had told Abbot Hygebald (abbot of a house in Lindsey) of how Bishop Cedd's soul had come from heaven with a host of angels, to fetch his brother's soul to heaven: Christine Rauer, *The Old English Martyrology: Edition, Translation and Commentary*, Cambridge, D. S. Brewer, 2013, §37, pp. 60–1. Stephen, Wilfrid's biographer, also commended Chad's virtues: *Vita S Wilfridi*, ch. 15, ed. Colgrave, pp. 32–3.

41 Bede, *HE*, V.2, pp. 456–9.

42 Bede, *HE*, III.25, pp. 294–309; Stephen, *Vita S. Wilfridi*, ch. 10, pp. 20–3.

43 Bede, *HE*, III.29, pp. 318-21.

44 Bede, *HE*, III.26, p. 308.

45 Bede, *Epistola ad Ecgberhtum*, §5, ed. and trans. Christopher Grocock and I. N. Wood, *Abbots of Wearmouth and Jarrow*, Oxford, Oxford University Press, 2013, pp. 124-61 (at 130-3).

46 Compare the provisions of the Council of *Clofesho* of 747, ch. 29, in Arthur West Haddan and William Stubbs (eds), *Councils and Ecclesiastical Documents Relating to Great Britain and Ireland*, 3 vols in 4, Oxford, Clarendon Press, 1868-78 (reprinted 1964), III.374-5; Catherine Cubitt, 'Pastoral Care and Conciliar Canons: The Provisions of the 747 Council of *Clofesho*', in John Blair and Richard Sharpe (eds), *Pastoral Care Before the Parish*, Leicester, Leicester University Press, 1992, pp. 193-211; Alan Thacker, 'Priests and Pastoral Care in Anglo-Saxon England', in George Hardin Brown and Linda E. Voigts (eds), *The Study of Medieval Manuscripts of England: Festschrift in Honor of Richard W. Pfaff*, Turnhout: Brepols, 2010, pp. 187-208 (at 199).

47 Bede, *Homelia* I.12, trans. Lawrence T. Martin and David Hurst, *Bede the Venerable: Homilies on the Gospels*, 2 vols, Kalamazoo, MI: Cistercian Publications, 1991, I.119.

48 Bede, *Homelia* I.20, trans. Martin and Hurst, *Homilies*, I.202; Thacker, 'Priests', p. 203.

49 Thacker, 'Bede's Ideal of Reform'.

50 Theodore, Penitential, I.xiv.28; II.ii.2, 3, 7, 9, 15, in Paul Willem Finsterwalder (ed.), *Die Canones Theodori Cantuariensis und ihre Überlieferungsformen*, Weimar: H. Böhlaus, 1929, pp. 310, 313-15; Council of *Clofesho*, AD 747, chs 8-11, in Haddan and Stubbs, *Councils*, III.365-6.

51 For general surveys of hermits in early Anglo-Saxon England, see Mary Clayton, 'Hermits and the Contemplative Life', in Paul E. Szarmach (ed.), *Holy Men and Holy Women: Old English Prose Saints' Lives and Their Contexts*, Albany, NY, SUNY P ress, 1996, pp. 147-75 (especially 153-6); John Blair, *The Church in Anglo-Saxon Society*, Oxford, Oxford University Press, 2005, pp. 216-20; and Tom Licence, *Hermits and Recluses in English Society 950-1200*, Oxford, Oxford University Press, 2011, pp. 22-7.

52 Bede, *HE*, III.19, pp. 274-7; Simon Coates, 'The Bishop as Pastor and Solitary: Bede and the Spiritual Authority of the Monk-Bishop', *Journal of Ecclesiastical History* 47 (1996), pp. 601-19 (at 607-8).

53 Anon., *Vita S. Cuthberti*, III.1, ed. and trans. Bertram Colgrave, *Two Lives of Saint Cuthbert*, Cambridge, Cambridge University Press, 1940, pp. 59-140 (at 94-7).

54 Bede, *Vita S. Cuthberti*, ch. 17, pp. 214-15.

55 Anon., *Vita S. Cuthberti*, III.2-7, pp. 96-108.

56 Anon., *Vita S. Cuthberti*, III.7, pp. 104-7; most of this chapter consists of direct quotation from the Life of Antony. On the literary models

for Cuthbert's sanctity, see Coates, 'The Bishop as Pastor and Solitary', pp. 612–16.

57 Clare Stancliffe, 'Cuthbert and the Polarity Between Pastor and Solitary', in Gerald Bonner, David Rollason and Clare Stancliffe (eds), *St Cuthbert, His Cult and His Community*, Woodbridge, Boydell & Brewer, 1989, pp. 21–44 (at 34–6).

58 Anon., *Vita S. Cuthberti*, IV.11, pp. 128–9; cf. Bede, *Vita S. Cuthberti*, chs 37–40, pp. 280–7.

59 Thacker, 'Bede's Ideal of Reform', pp. 134–42.

60 Bede, *HE*, III.19, pp. 276–7.

61 Felix, *Vita S. Guthlaci*, ch. 24, ed. and trans. Bertram Colgrave, *Felix's Life of Saint Guthlac*, Cambridge, Cambridge University Press, 1956 (new edn, 1985), pp. 86–7; Henry Mayr-Harting, 'Guthlac [St Guthlac] (674–715)', *Oxford Dictionary of National Biography*, Oxford, Oxford University Press, 2004.

62 Mayr-Harting, *The Coming*, pp. 237–9.

63 Felix, *Vita S. Guthlaci*, ch. 50, pp. 156–7. Little is known about Pega beyond the fragments reported by Felix and the preservation of her memory in the place-name Peakirk; see further Colgrave, *Felix*, pp. 192–3. Orderic Vitalis reported that Pega had lived at the monastery of Peakirk for many years until her brother's death; but then wanted to go on pilgrimage to Rome, in order to pray at the threshold of the Apostles. She died in that city and miracles were performed at the church where her relics were buried: *The Ecclesiastical History of Orderic Vitalis*, ed. and trans. Marjorie Chibnall, 6 vols, Oxford, Clarendon Press, 1969–80, II.342–5.

64 Felix, *Vita S Guthlaci*, ch. 51, pp. 162–3.

65 Stephen, *Vita S Wilfridi*, ch. 64, pp. 138–9.

66 Anon., *Vita S Ceolfridi*, ch. 2, ed. and trans. Grocock and Wood, pp. 78–121 (at 80–1).

67 Bede, *HE*, V.9, pp. 478–9.

68 Bede, *HE*, V.12, pp. 496–7.

69 Wilhelm Levison, *England and the Continent in the Eighth Century*, Oxford, Clarendon Press, 1946, p. 168.

70 Louis Gougaud, *Ermites et reclus*, Vienne, Ligugé, 1928, p. 81; Clayton, 'Hermits', p. 154.

71 Bede, *HE*, V.1, pp. 454–7; cf. also Bede, *Vita S Cuthberti*, ch. 46, pp. 302–3.

72 Bede, *Vita S Cuthberti*, ch. 46, pp. 302–5.

73 British Library, Cotton MS Nero D.IV, fo 259r; the colophon is discussed in T. D. Kendrick et al., *Evangeliorum quattuor Codex Lindisfarnensis*, 2 vols, Oltun et Lausanna Helvetiae, Urs Graf, 1956–60, II.5–11, 84; see David Rollason, 'Billfrith [St Billfrith] (d. 750x800?)', *Oxford Dictionary of National Biography*, Oxford, Oxford University Press, 2004.

74 Felgild and Billfrith were the other two named: Durham *Liber Vitae*: BL, Cotton MS Domitian vii, fo 18r.

75 *Historia Regum*, s.a. 756, ed. Thomas Arnold, 1882–85, *Symeonis monachi opera omnia*, 2 vols, London, Longman, II.41; Simeon of Durham, *Libellus de exordio atque procursu istius, hoc est Dunhelmensis, ecclesie = Tract on the origins and progress of this the Church of Durham*, II.2, ed. David Rollason, Oxford, Oxford University Press, 2000, pp. 80–1.

76 *Historia Regum*, s.a. 767, ed. Arnold, II. 43.

77 Licence, *Hermits*, pp. 25–6.

78 David Rollason, Lynda Rollason and Elizabeth Briggs, *The Durham Liber Vitae: London, British Library, MS Cotton Domitian A.VII: Edition and Digital Facsimile with Introduction, Codicological, Prosopographical and Linguistic Commentary, and Indexes*, 3 vols, London, British Library, 2007, III.84.

79 Levison, *England and the Continent*, pp. 295–302; A. B. Kuypers (ed.), *The Prayer Book of Aedeluald the Bishop, commonly called the Book of Cerne*, Cambridge, Cambridge University Press, 1902, pp. 143–5 and 155 (nos 47, 48 and 58); Michelle P. Brown, *The Book of Cerne: Prayer, Patronage and Power in Ninth-Century England*, London and Toronto: British Library, 1996, pp. 137, 140–1, 155.

80 Alcuin, *Versus de patribus, regibus et sanctis Euboricensis ecclesiae*, lines 1022–33, in Peter Godman, *The Bishops, Kings, and Saints of York*, Oxford, Clarendon Press, 1982, pp. 82–3.

81 Alcuin, *Versus*, lines 1319–87, pp. 104–9.

82 Alcuin, *Versus*, lines 1388–93, pp. 108–9.

83 Stephen, *Vita S Wilfridi*, ch. 62, pp. 134–5.

84 Blair, *The Church*, pp. 144–5, 216.

85 Alcuin, *Vita S Willibrordi*, ch. 1, in Wilhelm Levison (ed.), *Monumenta Germaniae Historica, Scriptores Rerum Germanicarum*, VII, Hanover and Leipzig, Hahn, 1920, pp. 81–141 (at 116).

86 Felix, *Vita S Guthlaci*, chs 35–49; Licence, *Hermits*, pp. 24–5.

87 Felix, *Vita S Guthlaci*, ch. 48, pp. 148–9; Licence, *Hermits*, p. 25.

88 Bede, *HE*, IV.29, pp. 440–3; cf. Anon., *Vita S Cuthberti*, IV.9, pp. 124–5.

89 Felix, *Vita S Guthlaci*, ch. 46, pp. 142–5.

90 Thacker, 'Priests and Pastoral Care', p. 203.

91 Thacker, 'Bede's Ideal of Reform', p. 132.

92 Thacker, 'Bede's Ideal of Reform', p. 141.

93 Bede, *Vita S Cuthberti*, ch. 22, pp. 228–31.

94 Bede, *Homelia*, I. 7, trans. Martin and Hurst, p. 66.

# 3

# Father William's Baton

## PETÀ DUNSTAN

### The revival of Anglican religious life

At the time of the Reformation in the sixteenth century, it appeared as if religious communities in Britain had been swept away for good, along with the ecclesiastical jurisdiction of Rome, as the Church of England forged a path independent of papal authority. The monasteries were dissolved and the religious orders banished. In the contemporary Protestant political mind, religious life was associated with the papal system and hence with Britain's major political and economic enemies: Spain and France. Both of those nations had remained staunchly Roman Catholic in their ecclesiastical allegiance. To this mindset therefore, to advocate religious life would be to advocate the rule of foreigners and a destruction of the liberties that the Reformation was judged to have brought. Those who had benefitted economically from the dissolution, for example by taking over former monastic land, had also much to lose if there was a restoration. The idea of a revival of communities was therefore socially and politically dangerous. Despite this, the echoes of religious life remained – in Oxford and Cambridge colleges, some almshouses and cathedrals – yet as a tradition disguised. Then, in the 1840s and 1850s, various factors came together to release a surge of spiritual energy that resulted in an open revival of religious life among Anglicans.

The main stimulus was the Industrial Revolution, accompanied by a numerical increase in population, luring many from the countryside into towns, which consequently grew into large cities. Factories mushroomed, pollution mounted. The hastily built slums to house this influx of workers became rife with disease, deprivation and misery. The pastoral challenge for the vicars of the parishes caught amid this swift economic and social change was enormous. Parliament provided funds to build new churches and create new parishes, but these needed staffing. Fresh ideas were sought and one was the revival of sisterhoods, who could minister to women and children in particular. Lutherans in Germany had founded a community of deaconesses at Kaiserswerth and this was an example that some felt should be followed. Many bishops therefore welcomed the idea of women's communities to provide a pool of dedicated parish workers to support the clergy. They remained wary of the structures of traditional religious life, most notably in their suspicion about anyone taking lifelong vows. Indeed, the status of any such vows provoked a controversy that simmered through the following decades, but this did not prevent some bishops from welcoming the revival of communities for the work they could expedite.

Another factor encouraging communities was the Oxford Movement, which began with Oxford dons in the 1830s seeking to protect the Church of England from political interference and liberal theology by returning for inspiration to the patristic period. Here they found monasticism as a given in the structure of the Church and began to see it not as a threat to the Church of England but as part of a supporting structure that could protect it. For them, reviving communities became a theological building-block in awakening the Church to the Catholic aspects of its heritage and thereby securing its future against the liberalism which they perceived as a major threat.

Yet for those who took up the call to revive the religious life among Anglicans, there was a significant element to the vocation beyond pastoral need, ecclesiastical politics and theological trends. That was the call to prayer and to a life dedicated to the same. The very first woman to take vows in the Church of England since the Reformation, Marian Rebecca Hughes (1817–1912) in 1841, at first envisaged a cloistered contemplative way of life. By the time she founded her community (1849), she had realized that the needs of the world were the primary call. For her, education was the pressing issue and the Society of the Holy and Undivided Trinity therefore developed an apostolate of running schools and teaching alongside the recitation of the divine office. She was also bowing to the climate of the times and understood that a purely contemplative lifestyle would not attract the backing of benefactors or the bishops. A life of 'usefulness' was seen as essential in order to elicit the necessary support.

Nevertheless, the contemplative call nagged at many of the professed religious among the cluster of new communities that were founded in the succeeding decades. Some superiors and founders acknowledged this by creating opportunities for sisters to lead a more hidden life. Mother Priscilla Lydia Sellon SHT (1821–76) established Ascot Priory, for example, where a more cloistered life was lived than in the urban houses. Yet it was not an enclosed community, since a nursing home, followed by a school, was run there and so considerable contact with the world outside remained, even if the sisters travelled beyond the convent grounds relatively little.

## Men's communities

The foundation of communities of men took longer to establish, one of the most significant reasons being that bishops were loath to allow those ordained to opt out of the parish system at a time when the demand for parish priests was so high. Richard Benson (1824–1915) founded the Society of St John the Evangelist in 1866 in Oxford and was supported by the local bishop; yet this support probably had much to do with Benson taking on a new parochial area in Cowley. However, while Benson and his brethren worked in a lively and demanding parish, their home life was far more austere, with a monastic rhythm and much silence. There was little fostering of any camaraderie and conversation was strictly limited. The atmosphere was geared to a contemplative spirit seeking God and not to that of a fraternal house of priest colleagues. Under Benson's leadership, the monastery was not so much a 'home' but was a second workplace where the demands made on the monk might be considered even greater than in the parish.

Benson himself was not in favour of communities wholly given to a life of cloistered prayer. He wrote, 'I would have the contemplative side of the mixed life developed as strongly as possible. I am afraid that in what is called the contemplative life contemplation is very apt to be minimized instead of being promoted.' He believed the times in which he lived were different from previous eras when the contemplative life would have been in his view more authentic. Benson continued later in the same letter,

... we have a duty towards the world around us. In former times people could do nothing for the world: they had to retire into the seclusion of the cloister to escape the world's wickedness. Now we have a vocation to bear witness to CHRIST in the world by active service. I should always fear that one who imagined she had a purely contemplative vocation was indulging a misshapen and self-pleasing idea. To the imagination it appears so much easier than a life of work in the world . . . The contemplative life should not be paralleled against the active. The active ought to have quite as much contemplation as the contemplative.[1]

There it was, Benson echoing Marian Hughes's position in 1849, but going further: the contemplative life was an integral part of the active, and now he added that if contemplation was separated from action it was 'misshapen and self-pleasing'. This was an unequivocal judgement from Benson that had implications for Anglican religious life. With SSJE being consulted for guidance by many of the women's communities, any desire among some to move to the purely contemplative vocation would not be encouraged. The pattern at this period was thus to go no further than combining a contemplative monastic life with a ministry, following Benson's SSJE model. The Community of Reparation to Jesus in the Blessed Sacrament, for example, founded in the poor area of Southwark in 1870, combined a sacrificial and exhausting ministry to the destitute classes outside the convent with intense periods of devotion before the Blessed Sacrament inside. There was to be no thought of enclosure or withdrawal from the ministry outside the convent. It was a challenging combination and for some decades CRJBS struggled both to attract and retain novices.

## The contemplative life

Only in the early twentieth century was this model seriously challenged among Anglican religious. Mother Elizabeth Slater CSC (1867–1949) was one of the most significant challengers. She had founded the Congregation of the Servants of Christ in 1897 to train missionaries for work overseas. After a breakdown in her health and a restorative trip to Switzerland in 1904, she became convinced that her small group of sisters were being led to a contemplative enclosed life and should phase out their missionary involvement. Her spiritual adviser, Father George Congreve SSJE (1835–1918), was not sympathetic: he shared Benson's doubts about an enclosed life.[2] Father George Hollings SSJE (1845–1914) would have been more so, as at the time he was bringing together the first women for an enclosed community in Oxford that developed into the Community of the Sisters of the Love of God, but Father Congreve did not share his brother's view. Instead he advocated that the Servants of Christ have a small retreat house in Essex where they could train novices and have periods of withdrawal, while continuing their original work for the Church at the training college in London. This adhered to the Benson model. Mother Elizabeth took his advice and secured a property in Pleshey but she intended that in time this retreat house would become the sisters' main home. She was determined to move on further with her vision as soon as practically possible and was confident enough to defy Father Congreve's advice, albeit with a diplomatic subtlety. By 1911, the sisters had swapped their grey habits for white, Father Congreve for the more sympathetic Father Robert Page SSJE (1839–1912), and the Servants of Christ had become an enclosed Cistercian-style community, with a few oblates to be their contact with the outside world. It was a journey to contemplative community life that would also be followed by the community at Baltonsborough, who adopted the Benedictine Rule in 1906 and evolved into an enclosed sisterhood.[3] A similar route was taken some years later by the Society of the Precious Blood.[4]

The model for the CSC retreat house in Essex had been taken by Father Congreve from a men's community: The Society of the Divine Compassion, the first Anglican Franciscan foundation begun in 1894 by Father James Adderley (1861–1942). Adderley's vision was of a community of wandering friars, who would spend half their time ministering to wayfarers on the roads and occasionally taking casual work, including teaching, while the other half of their life would be one of withdrawal at a quiet contemplative house. The prayer life of the latter would feed the intense activity of the former, while the active side of the life would inform the periods of prayer. It was a Franciscan variation on the Benson model: instead of leading an apostolic and contemplative life in parallel, this combined sustained periods of active ministry followed by periods of withdrawal. Adderley's early companions were more inclined to root the community of friars in an urban life, running a mission district and helping the residents fight for better conditions and wages, than have brothers roaming individually. Adderley, thwarted repeatedly by decisions made in chapter meetings where he was outvoted, eventually left in frustration in 1897.[5] His brothers, however, did found a house in the Essex countryside in 1905, a place where the novices in particular were formed in prayer before embarking on a ministry in the East End of London. It was this house at Stanford-le-Hope which was a parallel for Mother Elizabeth's foundation at Pleshey.

## Father William Sirr

One of the SDC fathers was a priest called William Sirr, who helped shape the life of the friary in Essex. Born in 1862, he had joined the community in 1902 aged 40. His previous experience led his brethren to profess him very quickly after a short novitiate, then make him novice master and put him in charge of the new Essex house. Sirr was known both for his sympathetic spiritual accompaniment and his unrelenting advocacy for the poor. SDC, following a community policy, would not have amenities (such as a bathroom) in its own friary that were absent from the homes of the poor around them. The brethren would spend time living alongside working-class families when they could, so that their understanding of conditions was first-hand, while some of the non-ordained brethren continued to work at their artisan crafts, trying to earn a living in the same way as their neighbours.

William Sirr had been born into a life of more privilege but then had found it snatched away by the events of his childhood. His father, (Henry) Charles Sirr (1807–72), came from a Dublin family. He had been a lawyer and worked overseas in Hong Kong and then Ceylon (now Sri Lanka), writing books about the people and culture of both places. William's mother, Louisa Rix (1834–1911), was from Norfolk and met his father while staying with relatives in London. She was half his age. There was much else that was unconventional about their marriage in terms of contemporary social mores, records showing that they married in 1861, a year after the birth of William's older brother.[6] There is evidence that his father needed to disentangle himself from a previous marriage. Soon after the children were born, and with the family living in

London, Charles Sirr found himself in considerable financial difficulties, another 'sin' in Victorian society, which regarded debt as a disgrace for a man, just as having a child out of wedlock would be for a woman. His hopes for educating his children were dashed, and he then died when William was only ten. This unconventional and insecure family background must have had an impact on the young William and was a factor in his compassion for those who did not conform to society's 'norms'. It also led him through his life to sit lightly to material comforts, and he approached many of the deprivations of life with humour rather than anxiety. It also led him to depend on God. His faith nurtured at Christ Church, Albany Street,[7] in London, was central to his life. Outside his paid employment, it was mission and other work for the church that dominated his schedule.

William had had to earn a living as soon as he was able and he took work in architects' offices, before at the age of 16 becoming secretary to a professor at the Slade School of Art. Already drawn to ordination, his family's lack of money made this aspiration beyond reach. Therefore, he had to find more lucrative work and save considerable funds so that he could pay for training at a later stage. Consequently, he took a better-paid position as a confidential clerk at a wine merchant's business. He saw much of the seedier side of commercial life during these years, and it meant that in later life there was little that could shock him. After eight years, he had accumulated the wherewithal to resign from his job and enter King's College, London, for theological training.

Ordination followed, but only after yet further tribulations. In his diaconate year, he failed his examinations for the priesthood and only the intervention of the Bishop of London allowed him to continue to the priesthood. The bishop realized that William's missional and pastoral gifts were more significant than his inability to master Latin. After a curacy in Vauxhall, William entered the Franciscan Society of the Divine Compassion in March 1902. Professed in October 1903 and made novice master, he was elected superior in 1906. His attraction to SDC was to live in a dedicated and sacrificial way, praying for and ministering to the poorest members of society. He had become a socialist in his political inclinations and believed the Church had to fight for the right to a decent life for all. He went on campaign marches and identified with the political and social struggles of the working class because he saw such a stance as an essential part of the Christian gospel. So, at this time, he was very much living the life of a friar. However, the busy years as superior led him to understand the need not only for action but also for undergirding prayer as its foundational support. For him, the Church could not fulfil its social mission without strong spiritual underpinnings. A call to a contemplative life grew in his heart and mind.

In 1911, the Bishop of St Albans, being seriously ill, asked Father William to take his place in the canonical Visitation to the Servants of Christ in Pleshey.[8] Meeting Mother Elizabeth, William immediately recognized a 'kindred spirit', someone who understood his own call and its importance for the Church and the world. She had also had to face much struggle to achieve her call, something which he sensed would be his own path too. Mother Elizabeth would play a significant role in William's life and vocation for the next 25 years until his death, a role that has been understated in the past. She remained one of his most loyal supporters, his 'hidden advisor' on many issues; his funds were managed in her name, and she was the most important of his executors until her death in 1949. There was ever a hope that were he to have established a community, it would have been the male equivalent of the Cistercian-inspired 'congregation' which was Elizabeth's goal.

## Sirr and the contemplative life

In 1912, the year after meeting Mother Elizabeth, William was able to step down from being SDC Superior. After a further period of reflection, he asked his successor if he could withdraw from active ministry. To test the call, in 1915 he was sent to SSJE's house in Oxford to live a contemplative and enclosed life for at least six months. Despite agreeing to this, the SDC chapter was wary of the request, especially as the community's numbers were becoming depleted by lay brothers leaving to join the forces in the First World War and some priest brethren leaving to join the Roman Catholic Church. SDC's caution was also influenced by the worrying precedent of the Benedictine community at Caldey Island. Benson's prescient caution was seen as justified by the saga of this men's community. Led by the flamboyant Aelred Carlyle

(1874–1955), they had developed a Rule and practices moving towards a Cistercian pattern and built an exotic monastery on the island. The idea that this was a contemplative community was stretching reality however, as Abbot Aelred spent much of his time away from the island pursuing financial donations and making contacts while cutting a grand figure. Leadership of the community of mainly young and inexperienced men was regularly left in the hands of an erudite and retiring oblate, Father Denys Prideaux (1864–1934), who lived in a guest house apart from the monks. The community was awash with ritual and rich liturgy, but it followed the warning of Benson's prophetic words: 'contemplation is very apt to be minimized instead of being promoted'. In 1913, in a blaze of publicity, the major part of the community converted to Roman Catholicism. This was a dire warning of how a 'contemplative' experiment could become disconnected from the church to which it belonged and exhibit instability in its witness.

No one thought Father William was anything like Abbot Aelred, but any new foundation would need to be carefully monitored. The remnant of the Caldey community restarted in May 1914 at Pershore in Worcestershire, but the only life-professed monk left the following year, and even before he did so it was suggested by the Superior of SSJE that Father William might take over. However, he was rightly wary of trying to establish a new community on the wreck of Caldey, especially as Father Denys was still resident and a major influence – and the latter's vision was of a Benedictine community with some ministry outside the monastery. The few men there were not attracted to the purely contemplative life.[9] Father William turned the suggestion down. He remained at Cowley for 18 months and after a further period helping his own community, he was finally allowed in 1918 to found a new monastery at Glasshampton in Worcestershire, in the neglected stable block of a long-gone country house. William hoped this would be the foundation of a community, but in the following decade and a half, while many sought his counsel and others stayed for periods of refuge, no other man was able to join him as a brother. In his late fifties when the monastery was founded and in his mid-sixties before the building's full conversion was completed, Father William was not at a stage of life where adaptation and flexibility were easy. Any cloistered community, however humble and sacrificial in its Rule, needs to provide a home for all its members, a sense of belonging so that they can live their call. Glasshampton under William's direction was not able to provide this. The monastery itself was impressive in its simplicity, the adaptations to the buildings paid for by a legacy willed to William for that specific purpose. His prayer life was exemplary, yet the office was recited so slowly that many found it impossible to tolerate. His practical skills were good, but his domestic skills less so, especially with respect to food, which was meagre and barely edible. Although he knew how to cook, he would 'just put food on and abandoned it in hope'.[10] His eccentric austerity therefore dominated the monastery, a place and its routines established by him alone without companions, and so it could not be easily shared by others for long. It was a hermitage for a holy man and, as Father William's biographer put it, 'Community life cannot begin with a Solitary.'[11] William remained a solitary religious, still technically a member of SDC until his death in 1937. Yet if William were not to prove a 'founder' like his dear friend Mother Elizabeth CSC, he was most definitely an inspirer of others.

William's executors sought to maintain his vision at Glasshampton, but after some false starts, eventually the monastery became a house of the Society of St Francis in 1947, where its novices could (and still do) undergo a period of training in prayer. In some ways, under SSF it has echoed the purpose of the friary at Stanford-le-Hope that William had established for SDC.

The contemplative life for men, however, needed to find expression elsewhere. Of the group on whom William had had most influence, two stand out as enablers of the continuation of his vision. One was Robert Cecil Sherwood Gofton-Salmond (1898–1979),[12] who did found a community but it did not flourish until he stepped down from leadership. He was from a naval family and had served in the military and studied at Oxford before being ordained a priest in 1922. In the early 1930s, he became a vicar in the East End of London, but his spiritual life followed a similar pattern to Father William's. His active ministry among the poor led him to believe in the urgent need for a more hidden support of prayer for the Church's mission. He began to live in a bungalow on some land at Crawley Down in Sussex in 1938, but the Second World War meant further progress towards a community life was slow. It was 1953 before Father Robert was professed and religious life began in a more regular way as the Community of the Servants of the Will of God. He stepped down as leader in 1965 and then, after his immediate successor was unable to persevere, the community was led from 1967 by Father Gregory CSWG (1930–2009), a younger monk from New Zealand. Father Gregory gave the community a much more defined identity and Rule, which included elements from the Orthodox tradition and led to CSWG increasing in numbers, including the admittance of women.

## Late developments

The other enabler was Gilbert Shaw (1886–1967), a married priest who never attempted to found a community but who evolved as a major influence on others living the contemplative life. Originally trained as a barrister, like his father before him, he then joined the armed forces in 1914. Invalided out of the First World War at an early stage, he did not return to the law, and after an abortive attempt to be a farmer, he was eventually ordained in the mid-1920s. For a considerable time before this, he had studied the contemplative tradition and was convinced that the Church required stronger foundations of prayer in order to thrive. His friendship with Father William began in 1919. Much of Father Gilbert's ministry was in retreats and spiritual direction, but the economic woes that followed from the worldwide stock market 'crash' of 1929 led him to realize, under Father William's influence, the need for apostolic work too. Father Gilbert went to live in Stepney in London, where, from a disused pub, he provided clothing and food, as well as using his legal knowledge to help in the struggle for fair rents, better housing and education. He met and then helped Father Robert at his church and so was involved in the latter's decision to go and live a life of prayer in Sussex, being the embryonic community's first warden until 1945. Father Gilbert went on to be the warden of the Sisters of the Love of God in Oxford in the 1960s until his death in 1967.

The links between these teachers of the contemplative religious life therefore weave through the first half of the twentieth century, with their contact providing influence back and forth, but the major link between them all is Father William.

It is complex to attempt to distil his teaching as so much of it was an exploration, a moving towards, rather than a fixed position or theology. He believed in the work of the Holy Spirit and that the work of the contemplative was not to seek what he or she asked of God but rather to wait upon God. The monk or nun could only rid themselves of distractions and obstacles which interfere with the bestowal of spiritual gifts from God, not seek the gifts for themselves. It was this sense of patience and humility that flowed through William's witness and made him so authentic to those who met him. He was not putting forward a spiritual plan or teaching others a technique of prayer. He advised and encouraged the clearing away of the emotional and spiritual debris that cluttered the individual soul, this being achieved through a path of repentance and forgiveness; then to await the gifts of God through prayer and silence. It was a challenging path, yet a simple one in its approach unhampered by mystical complexity.

This simplicity of approach also distanced him from the ecclesiastical squabbles and political manoeuvres that had so marred the Church's witness over the centuries. When faced with people troubled over converting to another Christian denomination, he was clear that such decisions were not the most important matters facing the individual soul: 'I know in my heart of hearts that all the baptized are in the Mystical Body of Christ.'[13] He was ecumenical long before any significant moves to reconciliation began among the churches in Britain. In this, he was illustrating how the monastic life could be a prophetic sign rising above what seemed at the time insuperable barriers to Christian companionship let alone unity.

His greatest gift, however, might be judged to be his example of the contemplative life as connected to the world and not as an escape or separation. His example was of a simple Christian life lived in an intense prayerful way, not an exotic and outlandish retreat from the ordinary. This is significant because the fear of those who opposed the cloistered life was that it was remote and mysterious, cultivating not just a detachment but a distance from the outside world. The talk of 'leaving the world' and taking on a new name, as if the 'old self' had died, was not the language of Father William. He kept his own name and remained in touch with his friends and contacts. He lived the same rhythm of life he had as an 'active' religious. He changed only in that he embraced a greater degree of silence and longer periods of prayer – and he stayed in one place. The quest of the contemplative for closer union with God was not an individual aspiration but a work on behalf of all humanity. So, for Father William, his life as a contemplative meant a detachment from the distractions of the world but not from concern for its sufferings. He was in regular touch with those who served the poor, encouraging a 'follower' such as Father Gilbert Shaw to seek work in that field when contemporary economic circumstances deteriorated. Many people visited Glasshampton and shared their experiences and fears with him, which gave him broad insight into the problems of society. One of his regular visitors, for example, was Stanley Baldwin (1867–1947), leader of the Conservative Party from 1923 to 1937, and UK prime minister for over half of those years. Baldwin lived nearby at Astley Hall and was a neighbour. Hence, Father William was never 'cut off' from ordinary life. In maintaining his connection with the world, he answered one of Benson's main criticisms of the purely contemplative vocation – and he had shown it could be done.

Although at the end of his life he did express some sense of 'failure' over leaving no ongoing community,[14] he never lost the conviction that the contemplative life was not just a hope for the Church of England but a necessity, even as his own life ebbed away. Therefore, while he did not leave a community, he certainly left the legacy of a profound challenge. With Father William's death, it was up to others to pursue his hopes and take up his baton.

## Notes

1 Undated letter, probably 1896, G. Congreve and W. Longridge (eds), *Letters of Richard Benson*, London, Mowbray, 1916, pp. 299–300. The capitalization is Benson's.

2 George Congreve, *The Interior Life and Other Addresses*, London, Mowbray, 1913, p. 182. I am grateful to the kindness of Father Luke Miller for this reference.

3 Now the community at Malling Abbey in Kent.

4 SPB was founded 1905 in Birmingham as an apostolic community, before moving to Burnham Abbey in Buckinghamshire to pursue a more contemplative pattern in 1915.

5 He tried to found another community but after a few years took a living in Birmingham and became a parish priest ministering to the poor in a deprived area.

6 Geoffrey Curtis CR in his biography of Father William puts the marriage as in 1859, but official records show this not to have been the case. His information may have arisen from Sirr family sensibilities when supplying information to the biographer. Public records also record a civil divorce between a Henry Charles Sirr and Penelope Mason in 1859.

7 It was in Camden. The church closed for Anglican worship in 1988 and later became St George's Greek Orthodox Cathedral.

8 Anonymous, *Mother Elizabeth: Foundress of the Congregation of the Servants of Christ*, privately produced, 1954, p. 26.

9 Father Denys was eventually professed as a monk himself and was elected the first abbot of the community that migrated to Nashdom in 1926. See relevant chapters of Petà Dunstan, *The Labour of Obedience*, London, Canterbury Press, 2009.

10 Geoffrey Curtis CR, *William of Glasshampton: Friar, Monk, Solitary, 1862–1937*, London, SPCK, 1947, p. 154.

11 Curtis, *William of Glasshampton*, p. 97.

12 His father was Robert Gofton Salmond (1851–1902). After the father's death, the younger Robert and his mother, Lucy (1856–1934), altered their surname to Gofton-Salmond.

13 Curtis, *William of Glasshampton*, p. 148.

14 Curtis, *William of Glasshampton*, pp. 156 and 157.

# 4

# Shepherds Law: The Story so Far

## STEPHEN PLATTEN

### The background

Whether it really was my first encounter with Brother Harold, I rather doubt, but certainly it was the most memorable early picture of him. Harold was in the saddle of his venerable 'sit up and beg' roadster bicycle. His habit had been hitched up and tucked into his knotted Franciscan cord and he was pedalling furiously from the Friary at Alnmouth towards Alnmouth station. This was in the mid-1960s, in the last days of steam when a notable locomotive was due to make its appearance on the east coast mainline on its way towards Edinburgh. Harold remains an avid railway enthusiast and it is but one side of his remarkable genius for embracing so many different interests and aspects of life, so many different personalities as his guests and friends, such a diversity of kaleidoscopic Christian traditions. All of this contributes to the persona of the friar (and later monk) through whom the phenomenon which is Shepherds Law has been born.

Even a fairly brief stay with Brother Harold at Shepherds Law will be illuminating. First there is the location. Looking out over the Breamish and Till flood plains, framed by the Cheviot Hills to the west and Ros Castle and Harehope Hill to the east, and focusing in the distance on the Lammermuir Hills within the Southern Uplands of Scotland, the view is breathtaking – the best view in England, some say. Then there is the folly farm which forms the background and perimeter of the monastery as it now is. A battlemented 'eyecatcher' encloses the remains of an eighteenth-century sheep farm up on the hills with the backdrop of forest and moorland and, more proximate still, a man-made reservoir concealed by a grassy carpet or overcoat. Some windswept trees remain, all that survive from a plantation designed to offer some protection from the wind, rain and – in the winter months – drifting snow. Here, then, is the stage set for this twentieth-century skete, offering at least a hint of the fierce and austere environment of the third- and fourth-century desert fathers, albeit in the very different climate of northern Egypt. All this is crowned by the modest nerve centre of the monastery in the house which is now the oldest building on the site, wherein kitchen, parlour and library nestle. Alongside this, cheek by jowl, stand the four two-storey cells of an almost Carthusian character where Harold himself and his procession of guests live, read and pray. Finally, just across the grass through an incipient cloister stands the splendid neo-Romanesque monastic church, winner of the 2015 RIBA/ACE award for recently constructed ecclesiastical buildings.[1]

But how did this vision of monastic life with strong elements of the eremitic tradition germinate? How has Brother Harold found himself living for more than 40 years in a semi-isolated location halfway up a north-Northumbrian hillside? The answer to these questions is intriguing and will also act as an introduction to the broader themes that this book will address, well beyond Shepherds Law. As we look to the background and roots of Shepherds Law as it has developed, so we shall on occasion allow Brother Harold to tell something of the story himself. This will set the scene for our broader discussion, but it will also offer insights into Harold's understanding of his own individual vocation. So, Harold reflects:

> The modern world has lost touch with the climate of prayer in which God makes himself known to us. Growing numbers of people today sense this lack, and places like Shepherds Law are there to keep the rumour of it alive, so that eventually people may come to find it again. Places like Shepherds Law are there for God alone, holding in being a climate of silence, simplicity and solitude, with – at the heart of it all – the life of liturgy and of prayer. This climate always transcends human boundaries, in a quest to live out the unity that is to come, with as inspiration and nourishment the life-giving tradition of the undivided Church.[2]

## Brother Harold's development
Brother Harold was born as Richard Palmer in Purley in suburban south London and is one of two sons of a businessman who became the managing director of the Properts polish business.

Properts made various shoe polishes and dubbins and were based in London's Battersea. Later the firm was sold to the Reckitt and Colman empire. Harold's first recollection of faith was being taken by his grandfather to see the Christmas crib at Rustington Church in Sussex; grandfather also read stories from Bunyan's *Pilgrim's Progress*. His faith was in the Reformed Protestant tradition, while Harold's mother and her family were Anglicans. Harold, who was baptized and was later at school in nearby Caterham, had a comfortable childhood; he went on to board at Bishops Stortford College in Hertfordshire. There were daily services at school, and Harold sang in the choir. On Sunday mornings the boys went to church in town, and in the evening there was a service in the school chapel. Brother Peter of the Society of St Francis presided at one of these services, an early encounter with the religious life for Harold. In May 1949, Harold travelled to Cambridge for a medical examination required for National Service. Following his encounter at school with Brother Peter, he lunched at the Society of St Francis' house in Lady Margaret Road. This was his first introduction to the religious life of the Franciscan community.

National Service for Harold was in the Royal Engineers. It included some time at Borden Camp in Hampshire, which afforded him the opportunity of working on the now defunct Longmoor Military Railway! It was also while he was completing his military service that he was prepared for confirmation by the chaplain; he was confirmed by Henry Montgomery Campbell, the redoubtable and oft-quoted Bishop of Guildford, in the garrison church at Aldershot. After National Service, Harold worked briefly for British Railways in Shrewsbury but after just a few months left, on account of colour blindness. He sang in the choir in Shrewsbury, where the organist had been a teacher at his first school near Croydon Aerodrome. Through this link he went on to teach mathematics at Highgate Junior School. There he remained for some five terms, and one of his pupils was the late Roger Kirkpatrick, who would eventually become Brother Damian of the Society of St Francis and indeed Minister Provincial of its European Province.

On leaving Highgate, Harold pursued further studies and cycled as a pilgrim to Italy, and notably Assisi. In the autumn of 1954, he began to study for a general degree in history and theology at Bede College, Durham. During his time there he experienced a difficult period of stress and breakdown, culminating in a deeper conversion in faith and then a period of healing. Out of this crisis issued his resolve to seek membership of the Society of St Francis in January 1957.

In 1959, as part of his time within the novitiate (the *enclosed* period of this novitiate), Harold spent time in the monastery at Glasshampton in Worcestershire; Glasshampton continues as a Franciscan friary where the emphasis remains more markedly on the contemplative and enclosed tradition within the religious life. The monastery had been founded many years earlier, in 1918, by Father William Sirr, of the Society of the Divine Compassion, to restore an enclosed form of the contemplative monastic life in the tradition of the Rule of St Benedict, a tradition which had been lost to the Church of England by the Henrician dissolution of the monasteries in the sixteenth century.[3] The reception of the Anglican community on Caldey Island in Wales into the Roman Catholic Church in 1913 finally prompted Father William into founding Glasshampton.[4] William was keen to root the monastic life in the wholeness of English Christian culture and tradition. This same emphasis is one which Harold has finally inherited. In 1937, Father William died and, to a large extent, his vision died with him. The Society of St Francis was invited to take over the monastery in 1947 and the *enclosed* element of William's inheritance survived in the part it played in the formation of generations of Franciscan friars. Indeed, while Harold served his term at Glasshampton, in 1959, the then novice master, Father Francis, inspired in him his love of the Gregorian tradition of plainsong for the daily offices and Mass, and also his awareness of the importance of prayer for Christian unity. All this awoke in Harold a desire for the contemplative and monastic life in the Church. It did so to such a degree that he asked for an extension of his period in Simple Profession while he considered the possibility of transfer to a community with a monastic vision. Harold comments:

This, however, was not to be, and with a somewhat heavy heart I made the Life Vows of the community in 1964.[5]

Harold spent some five years at Glasshampton and was then sent to the new house at Alnmouth in Northumberland. His dilemma was reinforced by a spirited debate in those years between those brothers who wished to press for a more contemplative life and those who saw a more active life as the main focus for the Society of St Francis. The two protagonists were Father Hugh for the more contemplative tradition and Father Michael (later Bishop Michael Fisher SSF) for the active cause of mission.[6] Michael's approach won out and it can well be argued that the active missionary life is more obviously characteristic of the Franciscan charism, albeit with a profound rooting in prayer. All hope for the contemplative life seemed to disappear for Harold at this point. What might follow?

## The ecumenical vision

It was the impact of the Second Vatican Council, beginning in October 1962 and concluding in 1965, which would rekindle his hopes. Pope John XXIII, in calling the council, talked of *aggiornamento* (transformation and modernization) within the Church. People spoke of Pope John 'opening the Vatican windows'. But it was Pope Paul VI who would make this vision become a reality.[7] In the two years that followed, through its constitutions and decrees, the Second Vatican Council effectively achieved changes and reforms which had taken other sister churches some 400 years to process. In looking to reform the Church itself, the council would also mean a turning outwards towards the world. Alongside the work of the council, that process and shift was reflected elsewhere in Pope Paul's pontificate, both in the development of an Ostpolitik opening up the Church to the communist bloc in Eastern Europe, and also in the Pope's cautiously permissive attitude to the growth of liberation theology and base communities, largely in Latin America. Each of these shifts had its impact on all churches, and Brother Harold has engaged with them throughout the years that have followed. *The Tablet* (his comic as he has often called it!) has been regular reading over recent decades and has kept him abreast of developments in the Roman Catholic Church.

It would be the Decree on Ecumenism, *Unitatis Redintegratio*, and the Constitution on the Liturgy, *Sacrosanctum Concilium*, which would have the greatest impact on Harold and his life as a religious. The first of these affirmed the Roman Catholic Church's commitment to the cause of Christian unity and would eventually result in the establishment of that body now known as the Pontifical Council for Promoting Christian Unity. The Constitution on the Liturgy presaged both the translation of the liturgy into the vernacular and also the reform of the texts. This all stood within the broader understanding of the 'liturgical movement', a movement inspired, among others, by a number of Roman Catholic theologians: Odo Casel and Romano Guardini were particular influences on the thinking behind Shepherds Law. It is no exaggeration to say that the present pattern enshrined in the contemporary daily office of the Church of England, *Common Worship: Daily Prayer*, owes much of its origin to conventions which began in Shepherds Law, tracing the daily office back to its roots.

Alongside this, the fresh ecumenical air, coupled with an opportunity to travel, took Harold both to Frère Jean Claude and the Capuchins in France (to whom we shall return later), to the Benedictine monastery at Bec in France and also to the ecumenical community at Taizé. A year later Harold visited the community at Chevetogne in Belgium, a community (like Taizé) specifically devoted to the healing of Christian divisions, and notably the divisions between Latin or Western, and Greek or Eastern Christianity. A conference at Christ Church, in Oxford, where Harold met Mother Mary Clare (of the Sisters of the Love of God at Fairacres in Oxford) was also formative. Their warden, Father Gilbert Shaw (a noted writer and practitioner on spiritual direction), had also been a disciple of Father William of Glasshampton. In 1969, Harold returned to Glasshampton with the intention of exploring a more contemplative form of the religious life.

Once again, however, this was a false start since there were no others wishing to explore a similar vocation. Also, immediately before this Harold had been encouraged to visit the Orthodox monasteries on Mount Athos. His response to this is best expressed in his own words:

Here my mind was stretched, for I encountered a form of contemplative silence which was not hedged around with the legalisms of the Latin mind. At the same time, I saw monks fulfilling the mystery of humanity in calling upon God and relating to him in prayer. Back at Glasshampton this led me to read more deeply in the writings of the monastic tradition which had flowed from its beginnings in the deserts of Egypt and Palestine.[8]

## Realizing the vision

Many of these episodes just described provide seeds for some of the later chapters in this book, notably in relation to sketes but also on the wider discussion of the eremitic life within the setting of religious communities more broadly. In collaboration with Mother Mary Clare, Harold produced a paper for the chapter of the Society of St Francis requesting permission to live as a hermit. In response to this, he was given leave to visit the Franciscan hermitages in the Apennines and elsewhere in Italy and also time to search for suitable sites for a hermitage in England. During this period, Harold visited four locations across England: on Exmoor, in the Shropshire Hills, on the North York Moors and, of course, in north Northumberland to the north-west of Alnwick. Indeed, in the summer of 1970, the present author accompanied him, with nothing but a surveyor's tape measure. That was the sum total of our professional equipment.

It would be this location to which Harold would finally be drawn, for reasons both serendipitous and perhaps providential. The starting point of this seminal journey had been the curate of the nearby village of Eglingham offering to drive Harold round the countryside seeking out a suitable empty dwelling. Seeing Shepherds Law on the hill, he asked the accompanying priest about it and, even though the priest dismissed it as a 'ruined shepherd's cottage', Harold said, 'Let's go up and have a look.' They climbed the hill and on making their way round the corner of the ruined buildings they entered what had clearly been the farmyard of a now disused hill sheep farm. Harold notes:

> Everything was in ruins and long abandoned, but I knew immediately that I had come to the place I was looking for. There was no house to live in and my second thought was to dismiss this idea as an impossibility with which I could not cope.[9]

Various things happened which emboldened Harold to pursue the idea. Words from a visiting sister gave him courage; quite separately, a parcel arrived containing a trowel, a square, a plumb line and a surveyor's measuring tape (doubtless the tape which I held with Harold on his second and more detailed exploratory visit); the French Capuchin friar referred to earlier stayed at the Friary in Alnmouth proposing the establishment of an ecumenical project of prayer for Christian unity. This final event provoked an initiative whereby Harold and Frère Jean Claude produced (with the assistance of Mother Mary Clare at Fairacres) a letter to each of their superiors suggesting that ecumenical hermitages should be established in England and France to serve Christ and his Church in the search for visible unity during this present age. The English hermitage would be at Shepherds Law.

The site might initially have appeared to be impractical. There were, however, some factors in its favour. First, only a few hundred yards up the hill from the ruins, there was a small covered reservoir which supplies the surrounding villages. This would make the supply of fresh water a relatively straightforward matter. Second, and partly on account of the need for access to the reservoir, there is a good trackway leading up to the abandoned farm. The track, running approximately eastwards from the road which runs from Bolton, past Titlington to Hedgeley and Beanley, is clearly part of an earlier route which was never adopted as a public highway, when roads came to be metalled in the late nineteenth and early twentieth centuries. Then there were some substantial protecting walls built in a mixture of gothic and classical style which would, with the small tree plantation, offer some protection on this exposed hillside. Access to the Glanton–Eglingham road was also fairly easy albeit down a steep hill. There was even a small quarry on that steep hillside from which the stone for Shepherds Law was hewn; that gave space for a tiny shed which housed Harold's bicycle in the early days.

The next issue was to explore with the owner of Shepherds Law and the land surrounding it, what the possibilities might be. The Guardian of Alnmouth Friary at the time, Brother Edward SSF, was well known in the county and on good terms with local landowners. Brother Edward, alongside Harry Bates, who was not only vicar of Eglingham but also conterminously Archdeacon of Lindisfarne, accompanied Brother Harold on a first visit to Sir Ralph Carr-Ellison, the owner of the site, who lived at nearby Hedgeley Hall.

Carr-Ellison was a significant figure in the county and someone with a strong community involvement. Alongside having been High Sheriff of Northumberland, he had also been chairman of Tyne-Tees Television, chairman of the board that oversaw the building of the great Kielder reservoir and indeed, on the national scene, chairman of the Automobile Association. He had an excellent pedigree in public service and so the auguries were good. He agreed that Shepherds Law might be developed as a hermitage dedicated both to prayer and to the healing of Christian divisions between Rome and Canterbury. Furthermore, he allowed a trust to be established which would set the property within his farmland to be on a long lease at a peppercorn rent. An architect, who was a friend of the friars, agreed to draw up a simple restoration plan for the ruined cottage and planning permission was granted by the local authority. The only proviso that the chapter of the Society of St Francis had made was that Brother Harold should earn money to pay for the work required to provide accommodation at Shepherds Law; accordingly, he went to work at a London hospital.

As all this proceeded, so Harold travelled to France to meet with the Paris Capuchin friars and visit some of their houses. He also met with the French Secretariat for Christian Unity who gained approval for the joint venture from the Vatican Secretariat in Rome. The equivalent to Shepherds Law was to be established in some abandoned farm buildings at La Roche Mabile, a small village close to Alençon in Normandy. So began the very rich twinning which continues to prosper some 40 years on. Later, practical circumstances in France meant a move for Frère Jean Claude, who now lives near a small Marian shrine not far from Foix in the foothills of the Pyrenees south of Toulouse.

Meanwhile things began to move forward at Shepherds Law. An old green mission caravan was towed on to the site and it would be fair to say that a similar vehicle has adorned the site ever since, providing some ancillary accommodation. Harold was supported throughout this early period by the Archdeacon of Lindisfarne, Harry Bates, and his family at Eglingham Vicarage. On both Sundays and Fridays, Harold would appear for Holy Communion and, around this pattern, was built a regime of Eucharist, then bath, then breakfast and finally walking the dog with Harry. The Bateses, both of whom are buried just inside the

churchyard gate at Eglingham, became great friends and supporters of Harold in the early years. Harry died in 1980.

Young people came to assist with the building of the permanent
accommodation. One of the great 'wall-builders' in the early days
was Paul Guiver, a theological student at Cuddesdon College near
Oxford. Paul later joined the Community of the Resurrection,
Mirfield and now as Father George Guiver CR he is a noted
author on the monastic life and indeed author of a classic book
on the daily office, which owes much to reflection and conversation at Shepherds Law.[10] Later, different parishes and churches
offered either financial or manual support. The congregation
at Portsmouth (Anglican) Cathedral contributed some funds to
costs at one stage. St Mary's, Monkseaton, under the leadership
of Father John Lowen, contributed much both in energy and in
material support. Sometimes, alongside their witness of prayer,
when staying at Shepherds Law, friars from the Society of St
Francis contributed in very practical ways: Brother Nathaniel
SSF almost single-handedly excavated and constructed the main
drainage cesspit! The first buildings constructed at Shepherds Law
used much of the stone which lay around on the site. Throughout
the entire period of development until the present day, Harold
himself has not baulked at engaging in the practical work. From
laundry to washing up and cleaning, to chopping logs and making
minor repairs – all this has been part of a day's work.

But crucial too, of course, has been a very different sort of
work, the work of God, the *opus Dei*, that is the central pattern of prayer from dawn until dusk including not only matins
and evensong or vespers, but the little hours and, of course, compline or night prayer. When there has been a priest available, the
Eucharist too has been celebrated, often beginning with the office
of sext at around noon. Moving on from his time as a Franciscan
friar, Harold began to develop a more contemplative and monastic liturgy to serve the life of prayer. This was founded essentially
on the work which Bishop Frere had completed for the Order
of the Holy Paraclete at Whitby. Frere, who was one of the two
co-founders of the Community of the Resurrection with Bishop
Charles Gore, was a pre-eminent Anglican liturgical scholar in
the early twentieth century.[11] The resulting liturgical pattern was
essentially a coming together of elements of the old contemplative

tradition of prayer with the forms and language of the Book of Common Prayer. The first chapel of the hermitage was set up in a small wooden hut placed near the caravan; with the help of Frère Jean Claude, this was replaced with a lean-to, built at the rear of the façade wall of the ruins and topped by a corrugated iron roof. This chapel, which did duty until 1979, had a stone altar and a large wooden lectern. It was heated with a paraffin stove, and an oil lamp from the church at Old Bewick[12] was provided by the parish. Thereafter the chapel was transferred into the roof space of the now completed dwelling house.

## The hermitage is consolidated

In the early 1980s, Harold decided – with the support of the recently appointed Bishop of Newcastle, Alec Graham – to remain at Shepherds Law and to develop the site in a more prominent manner with the construction of four cells, rather in the manner of Carthusian foundations. So the ground floor of each cell includes a kitchen/dining area; above is a bedroom with a tiny oratory and en suite facilities – there is also a desk for study beneath a large window on the south side. St Mary's Monkseaton was one of the main fundraising parishes, and the construction was completed by local builders, Michael and Eddie Pringle. The new cells were finished in 1989 and blessed by the then Archbishop of Canterbury, Robert Runcie. The Carthusian style of these cells offers a further insight into Harold's vision for life at Shepherds Law, which includes elements of the solitary life and of community life. So there is a strong element of the eremitic life there, but the intention has always been for there to be three or four monks living alongside each other, thus offering a creative tension between community living and the life of a 'pure' hermit. Throughout his time at Shepherds Law, Harold had conceived of a more integrated monastery, and so it was that the domestic oratory would give way to a larger chapel to the east of the main buildings and perhaps reached eventually by the beginnings of a cloister. Harold's mother left a legacy specifically earmarked for building the new chapel near to the entrance of the hermitage.

In the mid-1990s, Harold worked with a Newcastle architect, Ralph Pattisson (who had also designed the cells), to produce a design for the chapel. The foundations were laid in 1997 and the main structure was completed by 2004. The construction of the chapel was itself bordering on the miraculous. Although the legacy from Harold's mother was a generous gift, the construction was ultimately only made possible within the allowed budget by the reuse of stone found either at Shepherds Law or elsewhere locally. The builder was also local, Jim Donaldson, from Seahouses. He had been trained as a stonemason, and he worked with one or two colleagues. The crossing arches within the chapel were constructed on wooden frames and the 'fingering' around the arches owes something to Quarr and its French architect, Dom Paul Bellot, who was himself a monk within that community. The entrance from the narthex into the chapel itself is divided by a stone upright which was originally a dolerite whinstone gate pier from the local farm. The stained glass in the narthex and main chapel is by the architect, and the outstanding liturgical furnishings are by Taylor and Green, based locally in the village of Etal. The apsidal windows, designed by the Glaswegian artist Lorraine Lamond, depict the saints associated with the vision of Shepherds Law.

It was consecrated by the Archbishop of York, the Rt Revd Dr David Hope, on 18 September 2004, assisted by the then Bishops of Newcastle and Wakefield and the Vicar General of the Roman Catholic diocese of Hexham and Newcastle. Although there is some eclecticism in the design, the main architectural style is firmly within the Romanesque tradition; included, however, are details that speak to Shepherds Law's context. So the walls have within them fragments of brick, washed and polished by the tide at Lindisfarne; here is a clear pointer to Cuthbert, to whom the hermitage is dedicated alongside Our Lady. There is still detail to be completed in the chapel and possible plans for additions to its structure. As noted earlier, the design won jointly the RIBA/ACE award in 2015. The ancient–modern artistic sensibility Harold has shown in the design and furnishing of the building must in part derive from the artistic side of his family: the early twentieth-century painter Winifred Knights was his aunt.[13]

## A monastic liturgical life

Moving on then from buildings, we return to the developing liturgical and ecclesiological tradition at Shepherds Law. Again, Harold's own words may set the scene here. He writes:

But the most important revelations which life at Shepherds Law brought were not at all first perceived and understood. After some months I began to feel uncomfortable. Then I understood it as follows: I was in a cardboard box with SSF written on the outside of it. But the bottom of the box had just given way and I was in free fall. I came to see it as akin to Lewis Carroll's Alice falling down the rabbit hole; but what I landed in was an awareness of communion with the monastic saints of Northumberland who had lived a similar life in the centuries before the Reformation and the Dissolution of the Monasteries.[14]

This led to a reinterpretation of Harold's position. In pursuit of this he gained permission from the Minister Provincial of the Society of St Francis to approach Quarr Abbey on the Isle of Wight to see how the concept of stability and communion with a local tradition and the monastic way of life had been contextualized there. Quarr, a Benedictine monastery within the Solesmes congregation, had been the place of exile of the French community early in the twentieth century; it had thus not been involved in the controversies following the English Reformation. The then abbot, Dom Aelred Sillen, welcomed this initiative and Harold lived at Quarr for a number of weeks learning from community life and from the abbot himself. The large library there was also a key resource. Alongside this stood a discipline whereby Harold attended the local Anglican parish church of Holy Cross, Binsted on Sundays and major holy days.[15]

At the inception of Shepherds Law, Harold had been given permission by the SSF chapter to evolve a specific liturgy as appropriate. From the contextualized experience at Quarr (further visits followed) and the discipline of daily attendance at the liturgy, the *opus Dei*, arose the move towards using forms of prayer used by the monks of Durham to celebrate the festivals of St Cuthbert, their patron. Through study of the monastic liturgical literature at Durham, in the British Museum and at the Scottish National Library in Edinburgh, Harold began to gather together both the words and the musical texts which now underpin the rich and sometimes complex liturgical diet used daily and weekly at

Shepherds Law. The bringing together of this material has itself been an extraordinary and unique achievement.[16] This also stands behind the patronage of the hermitage, which is dedicated to St Mary and St Cuthbert.

The other key development that arose from Brother Harold's time at Quarr and indeed through his other travels and encounters was an ever-increasing and deeper understanding of the mystery of the Church and of Christ's prayer for the Church 'that it may be one that the world might believe'.[17] Shepherds Law was becoming a meeting place for Anglicans, Roman Catholics and Orthodox; indeed, Methodists and other free church men and women also had links. The hermitage was thus becoming something of an ecumenical centre in microcosm. It was, as Harold puts it himself: 'a neutral ground on which it was possible to appreciate spiritual treasures which normally lay beyond the boundaries of the separate denominations'.[18]

Throughout this time too, Harold's links with the Community of Transfiguration at Roslin in Edinburgh, and particularly with Father Roland Walls,[19] were also formative. This community had been founded by Roland Walls as an ecumenical religious initiative and included Anglicans, a Presbyterian minister and Roland himself, an Anglican priest who would eventually become a Roman Catholic. The community's buildings were based in a former miners' institute in the humblest of buildings, often described by visitors as 'glorified chicken huts'! Each of these different experiences and influences eventually persuaded Harold that the faith within him was, as he puts it himself, that of the 'undivided Church'. Harold notes:

> Without denying my upbringing, which had been begun by my Nonconformist grandfather telling me stories from John Bunyan's *Pilgrim's Progress*, or what I had subsequently received from the Society of St Francis, in 1996 I asked the Bishop of Hexham and Newcastle for the communion of the Catholic Church.[20]

This move was accomplished while still allowing Harold to live at Shepherds Law and indeed to continue to use the Anglican forms of the monastic tradition. The service of reception witnessed to a *continuity of life* at the hermitage. All such moves, of course, will be more difficult for some to accept than others, but overall the diaspora and local communities associated with Shepherds Law, Anglican, Roman Catholic and otherwise, have continued and indeed grown. The links with St Mary's Roman Catholic church at Whittingham have broadened local Roman Catholic support for Harold, and at least one of the trustees is, by coincidence, a Roman Catholic and another by nurture a Presbyterian. In contemporary language, then, Shepherds Law has become a place of *receptive ecumenism*; that is, somewhere where people of different churches can encounter and be enriched by traditions not present within their own communities. Perhaps most precious in this are the monastic traditions and within that, elements of the eremitic life. In all this, however, while treasuring most fondly the historic patterns of prayer and the contemplative life, Shepherds Law still points forward both to new and richer understandings of the monastic tradition and indeed to the 'coming great Church', when 'all shall be one that the world may believe'.

On the practical level, there are still things to be achieved. We have already noted that some aspects of the chapel remain unfinished. Then, also, the library is at present packed into too small a space for the number of books which have acceded to it. There is space to build a guest house for those who visit, and there are continuing practical needs such as a covered link to the church, space for a workshop and the like. The Friends of Shepherds Law are a key support, and funds have been raised to install a gas-fuelled kitchen stove and some electric lighting. Alongside the solar panels, another supporter of Harold's has contributed by supplying a diesel electric generator. On the human level, Harold still prays that one or two others might join him in this community eremitic life which he has pioneered.

## Seeds of a vision

It is Harold's witness, then, which has inspired the writing of this book. It is not a Festschrift in the more traditional academic sense, although the authors do both explicitly and implicitly pay tribute to Harold's witness. Instead, this book seeks to describe something of what has been achieved at Shepherds Law as a vivid illustration of what the monastic life has to offer to our world, but also to use this as the stimulant to further thought on how aspects of this work have been and may continue to be developed. As we have seen from Harold's own reflections, the climate of prayer is foreign to many, if not most, in our contemporary culture. The *raison d'être* for Shepherds Law stands, then, as a countercultural statement. Indeed, the difficulty in attracting others to such a pattern of prayer is a sign itself of the prophetic nature of the hermitage. Having said that, Harold's vocation stands four-square within an ecclesial vision. Both the ecumenical commitment and Harold's own journey are indications of just this.

However, the local or contextual is also crucial. Northumberland and Durham have nurtured the local traditions honouring Aidan, Cuthbert, Oswald, Wilfrid and others. Youth pilgrimages have been part of this tradition. Successive Lambeth Conferences have frequently included gatherings on Holy Island. In a symbolic way, people of a variety of traditions gathered on 20 March 1987, at the tiny chapel on Inner Farne, the earliest predecessors of which had been set up there by St Cuthbert, who had died on that same day 1,300 years earlier. The traditions of the 'double monastery' at Jarrow-Wearmouth, where Bede was a monk, and where he wrote his celebrated *Ecclesiastical History of England*,[21] the earliest such history, have also been formative. One copy of the Bible commissioned by Abbot Coelfrith survives as the *Codex Amiatinus* in the Laurentian library in Florence. The fusion of the sixth/seventh-century Irish and Roman missions to England following the Synod of Whitby made Northumbria effectively the 'cradle of English Christianity'. The missionary journeys of Aidan from Iona and Paulinus from Rome remain seminal in understanding Northumbrian Christianity. This fused tradition would be taken by Alcuin of York into mainland Europe via the court of Charlemagne. All of this remains strong in the northern memory and gives a fundamental foundation to Shepherds Law's identity.

We have already touched on the seminal nature of William of Glasshampton's work, not only in relation to Harold but more widely, albeit that Harold is perhaps his most important living disciple. The skete-like nature of Shepherds Law is also a witness to an ancient tradition reaching back to the desert fathers[22] and the sketes in the west of Ireland,[23] another link with the traditions of Iona. The skete, then, as seen on Mount Athos, is a different excrescence of the monastic life in small, often remote, houses. The pattern established at Shepherds Law offers a rich variety of points of departure in relation to the liturgical, monastic, cultural and musical traditions of the Christian Church. By its *radical* approach, using that word in its literal sense, it points forward to new possibilities, but rooted in the tradition, in a world which often appears to have lost the capacity or, at least, motivation for prayer and contemplation.

## Notes

1 This prize is offered jointly by the Royal Institute of British Architects and Art and Christian Enquiry on a five-yearly cycle. The 2015 prize was shared by Shepherds Law with the new Quaker Centre at Kingston upon Thames.

2 Brother Harold Palmer, 'The Hermitage of St Mary and St Cuthbert, Shepherds Law, Northumberland', unpublished paper, July 2009, p. 1.

3 See Chapter 3, Petà Dunstan in this volume, on Father William.

4 For further background on Father William, see Geoffrey Curtis CR, *William of Glasshampton: Friar, Monk, Solitary, 1862–1937*, London, SPCK, 1947.

5 Brother Harold, 'The Hermitage', p. 3.

6 Cf. Petà Dunstan, *This Poor Sort: History of the European Province of the Society of St Francis*, London, Darton, Longman & Todd, 1997.

7 Stephen Platten, 'An Anglican View of the Papacy Since Vatican II', *Journal of Anglican Studies* 14, no. 1 (2016), pp. 29–39; also cf. Stephen Platten, 'Selling a Tiara, Giving a Ring: Pope Paul VI's Jewelled Legacy', *Theology* 119, no. 6 (2016), pp. 407–16.

8 Brother Harold, 'The Hermitage', pp. 4–5.

9 Brother Harold, 'The Hermitage', pp. 5–6.

10 George Guiver CR, *Company of Voices*, London, SPCK, 1988, and Norwich, Canterbury Press, 2000.

11 Cf. Nicholas Stebbing and Benjamin Gordon-Taylor (eds), *Walter Frere: Scholar, Monk, Bishop*, Norwich, Canterbury Press, 2011.

12 Holy Trinity Church, Old Bewick, is situated about four miles north of Shepherds Law, outside the hamlet of Old Bewick. It is an eleventh/twelfth-century church and the chancel arch from that period survives. It was restored in the nineteenth century and consists of a small rectangular nave within a tiny apsidal chancel/sanctuary roofed by a semi-dome. Its remote location here made it popular with those seeking a place for silent prayer. There is a small wooden poustinia close to the churchyard gate.

13 During the summer of 2016, there was a retrospective exhibition of Winifred Knights' work at the Dulwich Picture Gallery in south London.

14 Brother Harold, 'The Hermitage', pp. 8–9.

15 At the time the parish priest was The Venerable Freddie Carpenter, who was also Archdeacon of the Isle of Wight, and a scholarly priest.

16 These musical texts have been photographed and the liturgical material typed up and stored electronically and in hard copy in order to make them more accessible and widely available.

17 To paraphrase. John 17, especially verses 20–21.

18 Brother Harold, 'The Hermitage', p. 11.

19 Cf. Ron Ferguson, *Mole Under the Fence*, Edinburgh, St Andrew Press, 2006 and John Miller, *A Simple Life: Roland Walls and the Community of the Transfiguration*, Edinburgh, St Andrew Press, 2014.

20 Brother Harold, 'The Hermitage', p. 12.

21 *The Venerable Bede, Ecclesiastical History of the English People*, Harmondsworth, Penguin, revised edition, 1990.

22 See, for example, Helen Waddell, *The Desert Fathers*, reprint, London, Vintage, 1998.

23 See, for example, Geoffrey Moorhouse, *Sun Dancing*, London, Weidenfeld & Nicholson, 1997.

# PART 2

# Unfolding the Mystery

# 5

# The Skete

## ANDREW LOUTH

In the traditional account of the origins of monasticism in fourth-century Egypt, there are identified three types of monasticism: the solitary or hermit, the communal monastery or coenobium (κοινόβιον [*koinobion*], from the Greek, κοινὸς βίος [*koinos bios*], common life), and the skete or lavra.[1] These three types of monasticism are associated with the figures of St Antony the Great, St Pakhomios and, for the skete or lavra, St Makarios the Great, the Egyptian (to distinguish him from his contemporary, Makarios of Alexandria, though they are often confused) and St Hilarion.

St Antony's form of monasticism was the pursuit of solitude; it might appear to be the original form of monasticism, as the terms monk, μοναχός [*monachos*], and monasticism are derived from the Greek word μόνος [*monos*], meaning single or alone, though these terms are later than the figures mentioned and only emerge towards the end of the fourth century. The purpose of solitude was to provide the stillness, ἡσυχία [*hēsychia*], necessary for prayer; only it was not as simple as that, as St Athanasios' *Life of St Antony* describes in graphic detail: the monk might, in solitude, leave the world behind him, but his mind and heart were populated with desires and longings, and fears and resentments, bound up with the world, which often seemed to be intensified, rather than diminished, by solitude. The monk came to realize, as Evagrios put it, that if, in the world, the devil fought with him through the paraphernalia of daily life, in solitude the devil engaged in hand-to-hand combat with the monk.[2]

In contrast, St Pakhomios' ideal of monasticism as life lived in common sees monasticism as consisting of praying and living together. There is allowance for private prayer, but stress is laid on the discipline of regular prayer together, in the monastic church, combined with manual work. The monastery is essentially a community, ruled by an abbot (with very much an iron hand, in Pakhomios' conception). It is a community, separated from the world by a wall. Entrance to the community is made difficult: a long period of waiting, learning by heart the psalms that form the basis of monastic common prayer. The wall symbolizes the separation of the monastic community from worldly society. The asceticism of the monastery is not a matter of, sometimes extreme, feats of fasting and other forms of individual asceticism, which often seem to characterize the solitary life, but the fundamental asceticism of living together with the brethren of the monastery, bending one's own will to one's brethren and the common life of the monastery.[3]

The skete, σκήτη [skētē], or lavra, λαύρα [laura], represents an ideal of the monastic life lying between these two extremes of the solitary life and the communal life. In its original form, it envisages a form of the monastic life in which monks pursue a solitary life, their cells (κελλία [kellia]) being separate from one another (maybe within earshot, but not side by side). They have a leader or superior, ἡγούμενος ([hēgoumenos] hegumen) or abbot, and gather together at weekends for common prayer and celebration of the Eucharist (a trace of this remains in the Byzantine lectionary, which has a separate sequence for Saturdays and Sundays from the sequence for weekdays). Such a form of monasticism is intended to combine the advantages of both the solitary and the communal forms of monasticism: each monk pursues a life of solitary prayer, but regularly meets with his brethren for the divine liturgy and Holy Communion, and has the benefit of a superior, from whom he can find guidance, and his brethren, from whom he finds support. The terms for this form of monasticism seem to derive from other languages (Coptic or Syriac) via Greek: σκήτη [skētē] derives either from the ancient name for the Wadi-el-Natrun, the desert of Sketis, where this intermediate form of the monastic life was first pursued by Makarios and his disciples, or is a diminutive of ἀσκητήριον [askētērion], [a place of] ascetic endeavour; λαύρα [laura] means a marketplace (modern Arabic souq) or a lane, the idea being that the cells of the monks open on to a common pathway that links them (the term lavra seems to be first found in accounts of Palestinian, not Egyptian, monasticism).

It should be noted, however, that in the course of time these terms, skete and lavra, have shown a tendency to migrate. Already in the early centuries, a lavra could mean a coenobion with cells for solitary monks attached; for instance the Monastery of St Saba (Mar Sava), on the Kidron ravine in the Judean Desert, retained its name of the Great Lavra when the present coenobium was established in the sixth century by the Emperor Justinian opposite the rows of caves which can still be seen and which were cells for the monks of the Great Lavra following the solitary life (originally on both sides of the ravine).[4] Nowadays, lavra is often another name for a coenobitic monastery, for example the Great Lavra on Mount Athos. Skete, for a long time now, can refer to a small monastery: for example, on the Holy Mountain a dependency of one of the ruling monasteries, all of which are (now) coenobitic.[5] Lavra, then, has really lost its original meaning, while the term skete still preserves the sense of a place where the life of solitary prayer is seen as central to the monastic vocation.

The history of Christian monasticism has been dominated by the tradition of the coenobium. This is particularly so in the West, where gradually, though not as quickly or completely as one might gather from many histories of monasticism written by Benedictine monks, monasticism came to be identified with the Rule of St Benedict. In the East, too, coenobitic monasticism has often proved dominant: St Basil, whose ascetical writings form one of the pillars of Orthodox monasticism, attacked the solitary life, famously remarking to the would-be hermit: 'Whose feet then will you wash?'[6] Nevertheless, Basil's own understanding of the monastic life grew out of a search for solitude and stillness, very much at the roots of the life of the skete.

Right at the beginning of Basil's (baptized) Christian life, after his attempts to observe the burgeoning monasticism of Syria and Palestine (he probably never made it to Egypt) in pursuit of Eustathios of Sebaste, whom he then admired, he sought a life of solitude and stillness. We learn about this from *Epistle* 2, which Basil sent to his friend, Gregory of Nazianzus, in about 359. The date and the recipient of the letter are significant; Basil had a little earlier written to Gregory celebrating the physical setting of his retreat in Pontos, to which he invites his friend Gregory whom he had abandoned in Athens:

There is a high mountain, covered with a thick forest, watered on its northerly side by cool and transparent streams. At its base is outstretched an evenly sloping plain, ever enriched by the moisture from the mountain. A forest of many-coloured and multifarious trees, a spontaneous growth surrounding the place, acts almost as a hedge to enclose it, so that even Kalypso's isle, which Homer seems to have admired above all others for its beauty, is insignificant as compared to this.[7]

And so on. Gregory eventually overcame his scruples and joined Basil in Pontos; but before joining Basil, he had replied to his friend's letter and received a response, which is preserved in Basil's correspondence as the second letter, the one already referred to. Gregory's response to Basil's account of the beauty of the place had been guarded; he had apparently said (Gregory's letter is lost) that he would rather learn something about Basil and his companions' 'habits and mode of life' than the beauty of the place – he wants to know about their τρόπος [tropos] rather than their τόπος [topos]. Basil commends Gregory for this, remarking that, though he could leave behind his life in the city, he has not yet been able 'to leave himself behind' (ep. 2.1). What is needed is separation from the world altogether, but what this means is not so much bodily separation, as separation from sympathy, fellow-feeling, with the body and its concerns, which include home, possessions, love of friends, social relations and even knowledge derived from human teaching. To this end solitude (ἐρημία [erēmia]) is very valuable, as it calms the passions and affords the reason leisure (σχολή [skolē]) (cf. ep. 2.2). Basil goes on to speak of the purifying of the soul, when it is deprived in solitude of the constant distraction of civil and family life. The soul is enabled to relinquish this world and 'to imitate on earth the anthems of angels' choirs; to hasten to prayer at the very break of the day, and to worship our Creator with hymns and songs' (ep. 2.2). The beginning of this purification of the soul is tranquillity (ἡσυχία [hēsychia]), which enables the soul to withdraw into itself and by itself to ascend to contemplation of God. For this, reading of and meditation on the Scriptures is valuable, for they contain not just precepts to follow, but examples to imitate. Prayer is stimulated by reading the Scriptures; it engenders in the soul a distinct conception of God, but more than that brings about the indwelling of God in the soul, for 'the indwelling of God is this – to hold God ever in memory, His shrine established within us' (*ep.* 2.3). There then follow reflections on the way of life that is conducive to this: reflections on the way we are to behave one towards another, with respect and courtesy, neither harsh towards others nor withdrawn; reflections on clothing, utilitarian, not ostentatious; food is to be simple and adequate, preceded and followed by prayer; sleep to be light.

There are several things that are striking about this. First of all, most of it could have been said by a pagan philosopher, talking about the higher life of thought: the emphasis on tranquillity, the sense of distance from the world ushering in proximity to heaven and heavenly beings; again, Basil's account of appropriate dress for the Christian ascetic recalls the accounts of the cynic philosophers. But the classical style and allusions are shot through with language that is distinctively Christian. Patrucco's fascinating commentary reveals, for example, that just after describing the Christian monk's dress in terms of the cynic philosopher, the term he uses – 'mourners', or 'those who grieve' (οἱ πενθοῦντες [*hoi penthountes*]) – is a word that had become a technical term for an ascetic in the Syrian tradition.[8] A more obvious example occurs right at the beginning of the letter, when Basil agrees with Gregory that solitude on its own is useless, because our minds remain cluttered, and says that we need 'to keep close to the footsteps of Him who pointed the way to salvation', and goes on to quote Matthew 16.24. Basil, then, seems to stand, quite unselfconsciously, at the interface between classical culture and the message of the gospel. But having said that, we must add: Basil is certainly facing in one direction – towards the Scriptures; there is a kind of turning point in the letter when he says, 'But the best way to the discovery of what is needed is meditation on the Scriptures inspired by God' (*ep.* 2.3). It was argued not long ago that it was his elder sister Macrina who brought home to him the crowning significance of the Scriptures.[9] Secondly, however, we find something else that is to become characteristic of Basil, namely the way in which our relationships with one another become themselves an ascetic way. For Basil, though the ascetic way involves an inward transformation, it is something that involves others, something that is tested and furthered by our relationships with other people. In this letter it is very striking, for however much the language recalls the ideal of the 'alone returning to the alone', the letter closes with several pages concerned with how we are to live together, how we are to behave one towards another.

This remarkable text – earlier, as a text, than anything we have about fourth-century Egyptian monasticism – reveals both the Basil of the later *Asketikon*, with his sharp question to the solitary, and a Basil who places the pursuit of prayer in stillness at the heart of the monastic life (to use an anachronistic term in this context, as the word μοναχός [*monachos*] was yet to be used of the ascetic).

Even in the West, the ideal of the life pursued in the skete was never completely lost or overlooked. Western monasticism, as we have seen, is overshadowed by Benedict and his *Regula*, which is almost entirely concerned with the life, lived in common in the monastery: there are details of the round of communal prayer, the *opus Dei*, the work of God, of the officers of the community, from the abbot down, and their responsibilities; there are chapters that deal with the purpose of this life of common prayer and work. There are the early chapters on obedience, silence and humility (*Regula* 5–7), the last of which, on humility, describes a ladder of humility, detailing the 12 rungs of the ladder; it is, however, a ladder, the sides of which are the monk's body and soul, which is made by fitting to the ladder the rungs, that is, the 12 degrees of humility, so that, at death, the monk may climb up the ladder to his heavenly reward. The degrees of humility are practical and largely concerned with the challenges of the common life to which the monk is committed: the sharp edges of his soul, so to speak, are smoothed over by the demands of living peaceably with the brethren. There is provision for private prayer, but it is parenthetical: Chapter 52, on the oratory of the monastery, where the *opus Dei* is performed, also mentions that it is a place for silent prayer, 'not in a loud voice, but with tears and fervour of heart'.[10] These practical concerns dominate the first 72 chapters of the Rule; and then follows the final chapter:

Chapter 73: That the full observance of justice is not established in this Rule.
This Rule has been written in order that, by practising it in monasteries, we may show that we have attained some degree

of virtue and the rudiments of monastic observance. But, for him who would hasten to the perfection of the monastic life, there are the teachings of the holy Fathers, by observing which a man is led to the summit of perfection. For what page or what utterance of the divinely inspired books of the Old and the New Testament is not a most unerring rule of human life? Or what book of the holy Catholic Fathers is not manifestly devoted to teaching us the straight road to our Creator? Then the Conferences of Cassian and his Institutes, and the Lives of the Fathers, as also the Rule of our holy father Basil: what else are they but tools for virtue for good-living and obedient monks? But we slothful, ill-living, and negligent people must blush for shame. Whoever, therefore, thou art that hastenest to thy heavenly country, fulfil first of all by the help of Christ this little Rule for beginners. And then at length, under God's protection, shalt thou attain those aforesaid loftier heights of wisdom and virtue.

The End of the Rule[11]

Or as Etienne Gilson remarked in his study of St Bernard: 'Fin de la Règle, qui signifie que la Règle n'a pas de fin': 'The end of the Rule, which means that the Rule has no end'. And he goes on to say:

The *Amen* of Saint Benedict has been understood. For to explain how Bernard has enriched with a mystical renaissance all those who abounded in the twelfth century, it is enough to grant that these final words [of the Rule] resounded in his soul as an irresistible call.[12]

This is from the first chapter of his book on the mystical theology of St Bernard, entitled 'Regula LXXIII'. Henry Mayr-Harting, in his chapter 'Benedictine Holiness' in a symposium on holiness, introduces his final section, a discussion of Dom Augustine Baker – the Benedictine chaplain of the seventeenth-century nuns of Cambrai (later of Stanbrook, now of Wass, not 100 miles south of Brother Harold's skete), who cherished and preserved the writings of the Middle English mystics, and whose teaching on prayer was based on them, especially *The Cloud of Unknowing* – by invoking the

ANDREW LOUTH

notion of 'Chapter-73-men'.[13] Both Gilson and Mayr-Harting
see Chapter 73 of the Rule of St Benedict as sanctioning, if not
requiring, the pursuit of a life of solitary prayer, within the context
of the communal Benedictine life, leading to the 'loftier heights
of wisdom and virtue': Gilson in the context of the development
within the Benedictine tradition of the Cistercian movement in
the twelfth century, which was renewed in the seventeenth century by Armand-Jean de Rancé, the founder of La Trappe; Mayr-
Harting in the context of the stress laid by Dom Augustine Baker
(an older contemporary of Rancé's) on the centrality of contemplative prayer in his guidance of the nuns under his care. Chapter
73 Benedictinism could be seen as a way of finding within the
Benedictine form of monasticism, which so dominated the history
of Western monasticism, the way of the skete. It was not the only
way: the Camaldolese and, especially, the Carthusians were likewise seeking the way of the skete, though in a strongly institutional form; furthermore, there were throughout the Middle Ages
and indeed later, not least in England, anchorites and anchoresses,
such as Julian of Norwich, who lived a life of secluded prayer in a
cell attached to a parish church, which made possible access to the
Eucharist and indeed availability for spiritual counsel.

In the East, however, the way of the skete – the provision of a
place for a life dedicated more fully to solitary prayer – retained
its role as one of the principal forms of the monastic life. There
must be many reasons why this is so, but one of them is certainly
the enormous importance for Orthodox monasticism of St John
of Sinai's *Ladder of Divine Ascent*. Although there is a wealth
of spiritual works in the Byzantine and Orthodox tradition –
the ascetical writings of St Basil, of Evagrios, of the fathers of
the fifth-century Gaza Desert, St Varsanouphios and St John, of
St Maximos the Confessor, of St Theodore the Studite, St Symeon
the New Theologian, of great ascetics and theologians associated
with Mount Athos, such as St Gregory of Sinai and St Gregory
Palamas, and later the ascetics of the Russian tradition, St Nil
Sorsky, St Serafim of Sarov, to mention but two, as well as the great
anthologies of monastic wisdom, the *Synagoge* of Paul Evergetinos
and, above all, the *Philokalia* of St Makarios of Corinth and St
Nikodimos of the Holy Mountain – John Climacus' *Ladder* stands
out: it is read, for example, in Orthodox monasteries during Lent

each year. Its importance in Orthodox monasticism stands comparison with the Rule of St Benedict in Western monasticism. Yet it is a very different book. Both indeed speak of a ladder, but (as I remarked earlier) Benedict's ladder of humility is something made throughout the course of the monk's life, rather than something to be climbed, step by step (there is not much sense of progress: each rung is as important as another). John's ladder marks out the progress of the monk's life, starting with renunciation, detachment, exile (ξενιτεία [*xeniteia*]), passing through the virtues to be practised and the passions to be struggled against, leading to union with God through the final rungs of stillness (ἡσυχία [*hēsychia*]), prayer (προσευχή [*proseuchē*]), dispassion (ἀπάθεια [*apatheia*]) and love (ἀγάπη [*agapē*]): it is a treatise on the spiritual life, in rather sharp contrast to the practical concerns of Benedict's Rule; or, put another way, it is an expansion of Benedict's *Regula* LXXIII.

Furthermore, and directly of concern in our discussion of the way of the skete, St John Climacus clearly favours the way of the skete. Towards the end of Chapter 1, he picks up the traditional theme of the three forms of the monastic life:

> All monastic life may be said to take one of three forms. There is the road of withdrawal and solitude for the spiritual athlete; there is the life of stillness (ἡσυχία [*hēsychia*]) shared with one or two others; there is the practice of living patiently in community. 'Turn neither to right nor left,' says the Preacher (Prov. 4.27), but rather follow the royal way. The second of the three ways is said to be suitable for many people. 'Woe to the man living alone when he falls into despondency or sleepiness, carelessness or despair, for then he has no one among men to lift him up.' This is what the Preacher says (Eccles. 4.10), and the Lord says, 'Where two or three are gathered together in my name, I am there in the midst of them' (Matt. 18.20).[14]

With this endorsement of the way of the skete, it is not surprising that it remained an honoured option among the ways of the monastic life in the Orthodox world. It can be traced, as an option, usually in connection with a coenobitic monastery, throughout the centuries; indeed, the normal monastic wisdom is that only a monk who has been trained in the communal life should embark on the solitary life, whether as a hermit or member of a skete, and John endorses this.[15] Throughout the Byzantine centuries, the way of the skete was popular, especially in mountains, not least the Holy Mountain of Athos (though it is the peninsula that is occupied by most of the monasteries). This way of the skete came to be called 'hesychasm', from ἡσυχία [hēsychia], the stillness and tranquillity of which St Basil had spoken: hesychast monks pursued the prayer of the heart, in which they came to experience the uncreated light of the Godhead. This aroused controversy at the beginning of the fourteenth century, in which the hesychasts were defended by, among others, St Gregory Palamas. With the revival of monasticism as Russia emerged from the Tatar yoke later on in the fourteenth century – a revival associated above all with St Sergius of Radonezh – hesychast monasticism assumed a dominant role.[16] The baton of hesychasm was taken up by St Nil Sorsky and passed to those monks, notably St Païssy Velichkovsky, who took part in the so-called Philokalic revival in the eighteenth century, which bore such magnificent fruits in nineteenth-century Russia, notably among the monks of Optina Pustyn. All this is a long story, too long to be dwelt on here, but there is one thread in the story that can be developed, at least a little. That concerns the prayer of the heart and the role of the Jesus Prayer in acquiring such prayer, which might well be regarded as one of the most glorious fruits of the way of the skete.

The skete provides space for solitude and prayer, but, as Basil had observed, solitude itself is not enough; it is not so easy to sever one's links with worldly concerns: through the imagination they continue to haunt the mind and draw it away from the tranquillity of prayer. The goal of solitary prayer has come to be called, in the Orthodox tradition, the prayer of the heart, and the way of prayer is to find a path, through the distraction caused by attachment to the manifold concerns of the world, to the heart. One way of finding the heart has been through the Jesus Prayer: the short prayer, usually in the form, 'Lord Jesus Christ, Son of God, have mercy on me, [a sinner]'. The history of this prayer is not easy to trace, mainly, I think, because its form and use came to be taken for granted, so that our sources are allusive and often maddeningly imprecise.[17]

Nevertheless, we can turn to St John Climacus once again, for it is with him that we find the notion of the 'remembrance of Jesus' in prayer, which is one of the roots of the developed notion of the Jesus Prayer.[18] In Step 15 of *The Ladder*, we read:

Let the remembrance of death and the single-phrase Jesus Prayer go to sleep with you and get up with you, for nothing helps you as these do when you are asleep.[19]

'Single-phrase' (μονολόγιστος [*monologistos*]) – from the time of Cassian, if not before, we find commendation of brief phrases used in prayer, sometimes from the Psalter: 'Lord, make haste to help me' was a favourite of Cassian's. The 'single-phrase Jesus Prayer' – μονολόγιστος Ἰησοῦ εὐχή [*monologistos Iēsou euchē*] – seems to be a prayer addressed to Jesus, though Climacus gives no definitive form, and seems to envisage several possible forms. The link with the remembrance of death suggests that Climacus saw the prayer as one of contrition and repentance. Another mention of the Jesus Prayer occurs in Step 21:

When you reach the spot, stretch out your hands and flog your enemies with the name of Jesus, since there is no stronger weapon in heaven or on earth.[20]

The context is the childish fear that may affect the monk when he enters a dark place alone: stretching out his arms in the form of the cross and calling on Jesus' name – both these suggest invocation of and reliance on, the power of the cross of Jesus.

The third, and most striking, passage comes in step 27, on ἡσυχία [*hēsychia*]:

Stillness (*hesychia*) is worshipping God unceasingly and waiting on him. Let the remembrance of Jesus be present with your every breath. Then indeed you will appreciate the value of stillness.[21]

These three passages combine three ideas, which are closely inter-related: first, ἡσυχία [*hēsychia*], stillness, the goal of the monastic, or indeed the Christian life, seen as 'worshipping God unceasingly

93

and waiting on him'; secondly, the obstacles to this stillness: fear and the 'enemies' – fear that is to be overcome by remembrance of death, for being able to face death overcomes fear, a fear that the 'enemies', the demons, seek to instil; thirdly, the name of Jesus, uttered or remembered, indeed remembered 'with your every breath' – meaning either a repetition of the name of Jesus, as in repetition of the Jesus Prayer, or a remembrance of Jesus so inward as to be as close to us as our breathing.

There seem to me to be two ways in which Climacus' ideas might be developed. One is by reflection on the role of demons. Climacus knew well the writings of the 'philosopher of the Desert', Evagrios of Pontos. In Evagrios' thought, demons, thoughts (λογισμοί [*logismoi*]) and passions go together: they appear inseparable – demons are assigned to each passion (as if they were specialists in one of the eight principal thoughts or passions – the origin of the Western notion of seven deadly sins), while the thoughts and passions seem interchangeable notions. It is the thoughts aroused by the passions that make the stillness necessary for prayer impossible. Evagrios' understanding of the way in which these thoughts operate displays considerable insight: the thought, or better, train of thought, associated with the passion of gluttony is not so much dreaming about splendid dishes denied the ascetic in the desert, but rather worries about the effect his regime of fasting and self-denial may have on his health. It is these trains of thought that invade the stillness and silence sought by the monk, and they are instilled and fostered by the demons. We have a word, *pandemonium*, which is significant here, for this senseless racket is indeed *all-demonic*, as the word's etymology indicates. To dispel the disturbance the demons are bent on, to control the passions and the trains of thought bound up with them, is a necessary, though difficult, step on the path of prayer. Later ascetic wisdom clarifies the suggestions of John Climacus by prescribing the gentle repetition of the Jesus Prayer as a means of inducing a sense of stillness that can keep at bay the disruption caused by the passions, by our obsessive attachment to the world and worldly concerns. Evagrios (and with him John Climacus) sees this gradual acquisition of stillness as leading first to an awareness of the world around us, robbed of our tendency to want to possess it, and able to appreciate it as it really is – in the eyes of God who created it. This is a stage called by the Byzantine ascetic tradition 'natural contemplation': the soul is enabled to see the created world as it is and to delight in it, rather than wanting to possess it and make it serve our own purposes. Understood like this, natural contemplation is not just a stage in the spiritual life, but an attitude to the created order that our society desperately needs to recover. There is a wonderful evocation of this in *The Way of a Pilgrim*, the nineteenth-century account of a search for unceasing prayer (cf. Climacus' 'worshipping God unceasingly') through the practice of the Jesus Prayer:

> And when with all this in mind I prayed with my heart, everything around me seemed delightful and marvellous. The trees, the grass, the birds, the earth, the air, the light seemed to be telling me that they existed for man's sake, that they witnessed to the love of God for man, that everything proved the love of God for man, that all things prayed to God and sang his praise.
>
> Thus it was that I came to understand what *The Philokalia* calls 'the knowledge of the speech of all creatures', and I saw the means by which converse could be held with God's creatures.[22]

Another way of developing Climacus' thoughts here is by considering the notion of the 'name', the name of Jesus. There is a danger that the Jesus Prayer will be thought of as some kind of *mantra*, the repetition of which induces some kind of spiritual state. The Jesus Prayer is, however, no *mantra*, but rather a prayer, addressed to Jesus who is called by his name. It is, therefore, a personal appeal to Jesus for his grace, his healing touch, his mercy. It also recalls a feature of the Byzantine or Orthodox liturgy so integral to it that it can be easily overlooked: the frequent, almost inexorable repetition throughout the services of the petition, Κύριε, ἐλέησον [*Kyrie, eleēson*] – Lord, have mercy. Repetition of this prayer provides a constant undercurrent to any Orthodox service, a constant rhythm, underlying and indeed supporting the movement of the service. The Jesus Prayer could be regarded as plugging into this; though repeated by an individual, it is not a prayer of isolation, but the prayer of the Church through an individual member of the Church. There are further associations of the notion of the name. Names are more than labels; they express something of the identity and uniqueness of everyone who bears a name.

Furthermore, the 'name of God' is an important theme in the Old Testament; where God has put his name is where he is present in grace and mercy, where he can be invoked: the tabernacle or tent that the people of Israel carried with them throughout their wanderings in the desert, the temple in Jerusalem, in both cases the place where God was to be worshipped. The name of God is wrapped in mystery in the Old Testament: it is represented by four consonants; it was only ever pronounced by the high priest in the temple, when he blessed the people – how it was pronounced is, for us nowadays, no more than a matter of scholarly conjecture (despite the confident use of 'Yahweh' in some translations of the Old Testament).

Invocation of the name of Jesus is, then, something special: an invocation in which we can be confident that God is present. Making a contrast between the sacral invocation of the name of God in the Old Testament – only by the high priest, only in the temple – Bulgakov declares:

> Thus, the Name Jesus has for us a completely unique and exclusive closeness and accessibility: if the Name of God in the Old Testament is terrible and miraculous, the Name Jesus is sweet, though mighty: in it we commune with God's love, we partake of the grace of the Divine Name . . .

and he goes on to say:

> . . . the Name Jesus allows itself to be invoked 'at every time and at every hour' and to dwell unceasingly in a person's heart. It is necessary to become aware of and to feel all the power and acuteness of this difference, even this oppositeness, between the Name of the transcendent God, which (according to the perfectly definite testimony of the Word of God) was remote and terrible and dwelled only in the temple, and the Name Jesus, the temple for which is every human heart, and every member of the faithful, as having this Name imprinted in his heart, is a priest of this temple. Of course, this Name remains terrible and, as the greatest of holinesses, demands for itself tremulous veneration, for it is truly the Name of God. But it has become close, accessible, not separated from us by the ontological chasm that

exists between the Creator and the creature. Over this chasm a bridge has been erected; the Divine and the human have become united without separation and without confusion: we repeat, only the priest or high priest . . . had access to the majesty of the Name of God, whereas the Name Jesus is accessible and is given to everyone who 'believes in His Name'.[23]

Which takes us back to the skete, for the skete is not properly to be regarded as a shrine, a kind of anchoritic temple, although sketes have throughout the ages attracted pilgrims, who have found there spiritual sustenance. St Maximos the Confessor speaks of the human being as a kind of workshop (ἐργαστήριον [*ergastērion*]) in which the 'divisions of being' (to adopt Eriugena's happy phrase) – the divisions between the intellectual and the material, heaven and earth, paradise and the world, male and female, even the division more fundamental than all these, between the uncreated and the created – are to be held together through mediation.[24] This cosmic role of the human, abandoned at the fall and restored through the incarnation, is nurtured and fostered in that workshop which is the human heart, where the name of Jesus is invoked in the practice of uninterrupted and unceasing prayer. It is of this that the skete is a symbol, for its whole purpose is to be that workshop in which the divisions that threaten to tear apart humanity and the world can be reconciled in the flame of the prayer of the heart.

## Notes

1 There are problems with the traditional account; for my take on it, see Andrew Louth, 'The Literature of the Monastic Movement', in Frances Young, Lewis Ayres and Andrew Louth (eds), *The Cambridge History of Early Christian Literature*, Cambridge, Cambridge University Press, 2004, pp. 373–81.

2 Evagrios, *Praktikos* 5 in *Evagrius of Pontus: the Greek Ascetic Corpus*, trans. Robert E. Sinkewicz, Oxford, Oxford University Press, 2003, p. 97.

3 On Pakhomios, see Henry Chadwick, 'Pachomios and the Idea of Sanctity', in Sergei Hackel (ed.), *The Byzantine Saint*, Studies Supplementary to Sobornost 5, London, Fellowship of St Alban and St Sergius, 1981, pp. 11–24.

4 For St Sabas and his Monastery, see Joseph Patrich, *Sabas, Leader of Palestinian Monasticism*, Washington, DC, Dumbarton Oaks, 1994, and Joseph Patrich (ed.), *The Sabaïte Heritage in the Orthodox Church*

*from the Fifth Century to the Present*, Orientalia Lovaniensia Analecta 98, Leuven, Peeters, 2001.

5  For sketes on the Holy Mountain, see Graham Speake, *Mount Athos: Renewal in Paradise*, New Haven, CT, Yale University Press, 2002, pp. 123–7, 224–30.

6  Basil the Great, *Regulae fusius tractatae* 7.4.35, trans. Anna M. Silvas, *The Asketikon of St Basil the Great*, Oxford Early Christian Studies, Oxford, Oxford University Press, 2005, p. 185.

7  Basil, *Ep.* 14.2, in St Basil, *The Letters*, I, trans. Roy F. Deffarari, London, Heinemann/Cambridge, MA, Harvard University Press, 1926, p. 107. I have used the text found in Basilio de Cesarea, *Le lettere*, I, ed. Marcella Forlin Patrucco, Corona Patrum, Turin: Società Editrice Internazionale, 1983, with its valuable commentary.

8  See Basilio di Cesare, *Le lettere*, I, p. 272.

9  Silvas, *Asketikon*, p. 70.

10  Translation, here and elsewhere, from *The Rule of St Benedict, in Latin and English*, trans. and ed. Abbot Justin McCann OSB, London, Burns & Oates, 1952.

11  McCann's translation has simply 'The End'; the Latin, however, is *Explicit Regula*, and Gilson's comment makes more sense if McCann's translation is expanded.

12  Etienne Gilson, *La Théologie mystique de saint Bernard*, Paris, Librairie philosophique J. Vrin, 1947, p. 26.

13  Henry Mayr-Harting, 'Benedictine Holiness', in Stephen C. Barton (ed.), *Holiness, Past and Present*, London, T&T, Clark, 2003, pp. 260–78 (at 272). I cannot believe that Mayr-Harting was unaware of Gilson's similar take on Chapter 73, though he makes no mention of it (maybe he knew it so well that it had become subliminal).

14  *Ladder* 1.47. I have used the translation (with occasional modifications) in John Climacus, *The Ladder of Divine Ascent*, trans. Colm Luibheid and Norman Russell, notes by Norman Russell, introduction by Kallistos Ware, Classics of Western Spirituality, London, SPCK, 1982 (here, pp. 79–80). For the Greek text, I have used the edition from a Athonite MS of Dionysiou, made by the hermit Sophronios, 2nd edn, Athens, Astir, 1979, which divides the text sometimes differently from the Migne edition followed by the English translation.

15  *Ladder* 4.68–72; Luibheid and Russell, p. 110.

16  This is one of the threads running through John Meyendorff's book, *Byzantium and the Rise of Russia*, Cambridge, Cambridge University Press, 1981. On Russian hesychasm (and especially St Nil Sorsky), see George A. Malony SJ, *Russian Hesychasm: The Spirituality of Nil Sorskij*, The Hague, Mouton, 1973.

17  On the Prayer of Jesus, see 'The Power of the Name: The Jesus Prayer in Orthodox Spirituality', Fairacres Publications no. 43, Oxford, Fairacres, 1974 (new edition, 1986). Reprinted in Elisabeth Behr-Sigel, *The Place*

*of the Heart: An Introduction to Orthodox Spirituality,* Torrance, CA, Oakwood Publications, 1992, pp. 135–73; also: A Monk of the Eastern Church, *Orthodox Spirituality,* London, SPCK, 1968.

18 For John Climacus and the Jesus prayer, see the discussion in Kallistos Ware's introduction to the translation of the *Ladder* in the Classics of Western Spirituality (see n. 14), pp. 43–54; on which my rather different treatment is based.

19 *Ladder,* 15.51; Luibheid and Russell, p. 178.

20 *Ladder,* 21 [20.6]; Luibheid and Russell, p. 200.

21 *Ladder,* 27 [3.25–6]; Luibheid and Russell, pp. 269–70.

22 *The Way of a Pilgrim,* trans. R. M. French, London, Philip Allan, 1930, p. 45.

23 Sergius Bulgakov, *Icons and the Name of God,* trans. Boris Jakim, Grand Rapids, MI, Eerdmans, 2012, pp. 156–7 (the English translation consists of a translation of *The Icon and its Veneration* [1931], and the last chapter of *The Philosophy of the Name* [1953]). The citation at the beginning of the second paragraph is from the Prayer of the Hours, which I have modified to the usual form in which it is found in English.

24 See Maximos the Confessor, *Ambigua* 41, in *Patrologia Graeca* 91:1305AB.

# 6

# Francis of Assisi: A Hermit and His Hermitages

## BROTHER NICHOLAS ALAN WORSSAM SSF

### Francis: urban or eremitic?

In the Upper Church of the Basilica of Saint Francis in Assisi
(c.1181–1226), there is a series of frescoes, once thought to be by
Giotto but now generally regarded to be by a series of anonymous master painters.[1] The frescoes, probably painted in the fourteenth century, depict the life of Saint Francis as narrated by the
Franciscan Minister General St Bonaventure in his *Major Legend
of St Francis*. The picture that I would like to draw the reader's
attention to here is no. 10, the Exorcism of the Demons at Arezzo.
This picture provides more than one visual clue to help us consider the attitude of Francis of Assisi towards towns and cities,
and his commitment to contemplative prayer in remote locations.
Was the innovation of St Francis the move from large enclosed
monasteries in wilderness areas – typical settings for Cistercian
monasteries such as Rievaulx or Fountains Abbey in Yorkshire –
into the rapidly growing towns and cities? Or was Francis by
nature more of a solitary, a hermit drawn almost against his will
into preaching missions, but most at home in the seclusion of an
isolated hermitage?

To begin with the first question, to establish the credentials of
Francis as an urban missionary, there is a popular view that the
rise of the friars, whether Franciscan, Dominican or any of the
other various orders, was essentially an urban phenomenon. R. W.
Southern says that: 'Wherever there was a town there were friars;
and without a town there were no friars.'[2] This was a view that
was already current in the Middle Ages, as shown by a popular

Latin verse: *Bernardus valles, montes Benedictus amabat, Oppida Franciscus, celebres Dominicus urbes.* 'Bernard liked the valleys, Benedict the hills, Francis the towns, Dominic the cities of renown.'[3] Traditionally, Benedictine and Cistercian monasteries had been built in remote places, like the hill of Benedict's monastery at Monte Cassino, or the valley of Bernard's Clairvaux; but the friars frequently found their place in the towns and cities that were growing so rapidly in the thirteenth and fourteenth centuries. For example, when the Franciscans first moved into France they went straight to Paris, famous as a university town;[4] and the English mission first established houses in Canterbury, London and Oxford, the ecclesiastical, administrative and academic centres of the day.[5]

Why did they head for the towns and not for the hills, as religious communities had so often done before? Southern suggests three reasons:

> The friars by contrast [with the Augustinian canons already established in urban areas] came to the towns, not for the churches or tithes, but because it was in the towns that they could find the people for whom they had a message, from whom they drew their earliest recruits, and on whom they depended for their means of life.[6]

The parish clergy were often unable to meet the pastoral and intellectual needs of the rising urban populations, so the friars stepped into the void, sometimes experiencing the opposition of the existing clergy who felt that their support base was being eroded.[7] The central ministries of the friars were preaching, hearing confessions, giving spiritual direction and supporting confraternities for the laity to encourage mutual support and charitable activities.[8] The friars were rewarded by the generosity of the laity in providing accommodation, often close to the city walls; and new recruits were found both among the restless, increasingly literate laity and from scholars at the universities. The scholars found in the mendicant orders the opportunity to step off the frantic climb up the ladder of ecclesiastical preferment in the search for financial security.[9] As friars they could forget about earning a living and devote themselves to the pursuit of academic study without distraction.

Francis himself, however, longed for the solitude and silence of caves and mountain hermitages, while others in the order were intent on establishing friaries in the towns where pastoral work and study took priority. Francis consistently prioritized prayer over active ministry. Indeed, one of the earliest Franciscan houses of study, in the university town of Bologna, was closed by Francis as soon as he heard about it, and the resident friars, whether healthy or sick, were thrown out on to the street.[10] Nonetheless, many of his followers in the Order of Friars Minor found the call of the towns and cities irresistible. As Humbert of Romans, a Dominican friar, said: 'There preaching is more efficacious because there are more people and the need is greater, for in the city there are more sins.'[11]

## Contemplative Franciscan witness

Although the friars indeed became a largely urban phenom-enon, was this really the plan of St Francis? Did he love the towns, as the motto above suggests? If we look at our fresco of the demons of Arezzo, we get a slightly different picture. There Francis is depicted well outside the city, exorcizing the demons from afar. Thomas of Celano, who first narrates the story, says that Francis 'received hospitality in a neighbourhood outside the city walls'.[12] From there he gets Brother Sylvester to perform the exorcism, while he himself remains at a distance exercising theurgic power by his prayers. The people of the town them-selves seem to be huddling behind closed doors, not quite sure what to make of these strange men who have just wandered in from the woods.

Celano often describes Francis as a hermit[13] retiring to deserted places to pray, only making forays into the towns to beg for food or to preach:

> He was not reluctant, when he discerned the time was right, to involve himself in the affairs of his neighbours, and attend to their salvation. [But] his safest haven was prayer . . . He would spend the night alone praying in abandoned churches and in deserted places where, with the protection of divine grace, he overcame his soul's many fears and anxieties.[14]

This had been the pattern of his life since the beginning of his conversion. While still living in his family home, Francis went with a companion to remote places where they could talk about the 'great and valuable treasure' he had found:

> There was a cave near the city where they often went and talked together about the treasure. The man of God, who was already holy because of his holy intention, was accustomed to enter the cave, while his companion waited outside, and inspired by a new and extraordinary spirit he would pray to his Father in secret . . . he was burning inwardly with a divine fire, and he was unable to conceal outwardly the flame kindled in his soul . . . Therefore, when he came back out to his companion, he was so exhausted from his struggle that one person seemed to have entered, and another to have come out.[15]

This description echoes the classic story of Antony the Great, the first hermit of the Egyptian deserts, as retold by Athanasius. Antony would wrestle with demons in the tombs where he prayed and kept vigil through the night, being carried out exhausted by his followers the morning after.

Francis loved to pray in hidden places, especially isolated huts or caves. Visiting the Franciscan hermitages today in the Rieti valley south of Assisi, almost every one has a sign to 'the cave of St Francis'. At the Carceri, the hermitage on the hillside above Assisi, there is also a hollow in the rock where Francis is supposed to have slept and prayed. Maybe he was entering a kind of underground womb, communing with God in the shelter of the belly of his 'sister Mother Earth', as he writes in his Canticle of the Creatures. Solitude and silence, hiddenness from the gaze of the world, were at the core of his journey into God. One humorous example of someone trying to break into the solitude of St Francis is found in the *Assisi Compilation*:

> One time when blessed Francis was at that same place, he stayed at prayer in the cell that was in the back, behind the house. One day while he was staying in it, the bishop of Assisi came to see him. It happened that as he came into the house, he knocked on the door to approach blessed Francis. He opened the door

himself, and immediately entered the cell in which there was another small cell made of mats where blessed Francis stayed. And because he knew that the holy father treated him with friendliness and love, he entered without hesitation, and opened for himself the little cell of mats to see him. As he quickly stuck his head inside the little cell, all of a sudden, by the will of the Lord, because he was not worthy to see him, he was forcefully pushed outside, willy-nilly, stumbling backwards. He immediately came outside the cell, trembling and stunned, and told the brothers of his fault, and said that he was sorry for coming there that day.[16]

Soon after this time of inner searching Francis made a very public renunciation of his home and family, and set off to find shelter in the ruined church of San Damiano outside the walls of Assisi. This is the place where the cave he visited at this turning point in his life is commemorated, and today a chapel is set aside by the OFM friars for contemplative prayer. Already Francis self-identified as a hermit: 'While he was completing the church of San Damiano, blessed Francis wore the habit of a hermit: a staff in his hand, shoes on his feet, and a leather belt around his waist.'[17] Not long after this, in response to hearing at Mass the Gospel reading from Matthew 10.9–10 about taking nothing for the journey, neither money nor purse, stick nor shoes, Francis renounced these outward signs, going barefoot and girding his simple tunic with a cord. In this way, he preferred the form of the gospel to a contemporary form of the hermit identity, but it was evidence of his practical response to the good news of the kingdom of heaven. He saw his calling from God as a command to live the gospel, to enact it in a radical, literal way rather than preach the gospel with words. The *Legend of the Three Companions* continues with his exhortation to the first six brothers:

Dearest Brothers, let us consider our vocation, to which God has mercifully called us, not only for our own good, but for the salvation of many. We are to go throughout the world, encouraging everyone, more by deed than by word, to do penance for their sins and to recall the commandments of God.[18]

It was a call to 'go throughout the world' (one might add, 'establishing hermitages and simple dwellings') not as prelates to exercise authority over others, or as learned preachers of theology to inspire admiration among the crowds, but simply as people dedicated to a life of penance, living the gospel, seeking first the kingdom of God.

## Hermitages

Later Francis moved to the woodland chapel of St Mary of the Angels, living with his brothers in simple wooden dwellings. This friary, known as the Portiuncula, became the favourite dwelling place of St Francis. He wanted this to be a model friary for the whole order, and at the end of his life he reminisced about how the friars once lived there and shared his dream of how they should live there again:

Our old brothers did this: for although the place itself is holy, beloved and chosen by Christ and the glorious Virgin, they preserved its holiness with constant prayer day and night and by constant silence. And if, at times, they spoke after the time established for silence, they discussed with the greatest devotion and decorum matters pertaining to the praise of God and the salvation of souls. If it happened, and it rarely did, that someone began to utter useless or idle words, immediately he was corrected by another brother. They used to mortify the flesh not only by fasting, but also by many vigils, by cold, nakedness, and manual labour. In order not to remain idle, they very frequently went and helped poor people in their fields, and sometimes these people would give them some bread for the love of God . . .[19]

It is essentially a description of a hermitage, where the brothers are devoted to a life of silence, fasting, prayer and manual labour. It is not a complete enclosure, as the brothers are allowed to go out to work in the fields alongside the farm workers. The work is chiefly to avoid idleness, but might also lead to donations of bread, the receipt of money being strictly prohibited by Chapter 4 of the Later Rule (1223). There is no prohibition on talking to the laypeople in the fields, presumably as long as their words are not 'idle', but there is a prohibition on the laity, or indeed other brothers, entering the friary, as Francis goes on to say in the *Mirror of Perfection*:

> I also wish that none of the brothers or any other person enter that place except the general minister and the brothers who serve them. And they [the ordained brothers] may not speak to anyone except the brothers who serve them and to the minister when he visits them.
>
> . . . I particularly want no one else to enter that place, so that they may better preserve their purity and holiness. Let nothing at all be done or said there that is not edifying, but let this entire place be held pure and holy in hymns and praises of the Lord.[20]

For those of us living in friaries today, sometimes overwhelmed by the number of retreatants and visitors, these are welcome words! For Francis, a place of enclosure was to be encouraged, for the brothers and not just for the community of 'Poor Ladies' founded by his friend and disciple St Clare at the monastery of San Damiano. Francis wanted his brothers also to experience the silence and solitude, albeit in community, that he found to be so essential to his own spiritual well-being.[21]

Probably the clearest example of the attitude of Francis towards an eremitical life is found in his writing of *A Rule for Hermitages*. This text, found in the earliest collection of his writings, was probably written between 1217 and 1221.[22] As such it is one of the earliest, and I would say most significant, of the writings of St Francis. It is a short text, and bears quotation in full:

> Let those who wish to stay in hermitages in a religious way be three brothers, or, at the most, four; let two of these be 'the mother' and have two 'sons' or at least one. Let the two who are 'mothers' keep the life of Martha and the two 'sons' the life of Mary and let them have one enclosure in which each one may have his cell in which he may pray and sleep.
>
> And let them always recite Compline of the day immediately after sunset and strive to maintain silence, recite their Hours, rise for matins, and seek first the kingdom of God and His justice. And let them recite Prime at the proper hour and, after Terce, they may end their silence, speak with and go to their mothers.

And when it pleases them, they can beg alms from them as poor little ones out of love of the Lord God. And afterwards let them recite Sext, None and at the proper hour, Vespers. And they may not permit anyone to enter or eat in the enclosure where they dwell. Let those brothers who are the 'mothers' strive to stay far from everyone and, because of obedience to their minister, protect their 'sons' from everyone so that no one can speak with them. And those 'sons' may not talk with anyone except with their 'mothers' and with the minister and his custodian when it pleases them to visit with the Lord's blessing.

The 'sons', however, may periodically assume the role of the 'mothers', taking turns for a time as they have mutually decided. Let them strive to observe conscientiously and eagerly everything mentioned above.[23]

A number of items mentioned here are worth exploring further.[24] The text begins: 'Let those who wish to stay in hermitages in a religious way . . .' This was a way of life that Francis hoped some of his brothers would choose, but which he did not expect all to follow. He realized that many friars would want to be with the poor in the towns and cities, but he also wanted some at least to be in remote rural areas. In part this was 'so that they [the friars] may better preserve their purity and holiness' as seen in relation to the description of the Portiuncula above; but it was also to enable the laity to have contact with and learn from the example of the brothers in all places where the people lived.

Thomas of Celano, the earliest biographer of Francis, saw this in terms of the friars themselves being the object of charity: 'The holy Father wanted the brothers to dwell not only in cities, but also in the hermitages, so that people everywhere might be given the opportunity for merit . . .'[25] Thomas writes this in the context of the virtue of almsgiving. He is saying, not so much that the brothers might be given the opportunity to make merit by living a holy life, but that the rural laity might fulfil the gospel injunction to feed 'one of the least of these who are members of my family' (i.e. the Friars Minor or 'Lesser Brothers', cf. Matt. 25.40) and so save their souls. Poverty awakens generosity, which in turn leads to salvation by fulfilling the teaching of Jesus to participate in the generosity of God by ministering to him in the poor, the sick and the hungry.[26] In any case, the life of the friars was a mixed economy: the distinctiveness of the Franciscan friars was not so much that they became urbanites, abandoning the remote rural monasteries for life in the bustling towns, but rather that they became a bridge between the two, inhabiting both the woods and the towns.

## The Rule for Hermitages

In his *Rule for Hermitages* Francis stipulates that there should be 'three brothers, or, at the most, four'. He wanted there to be only a few brothers together chiefly on the grounds of poverty. *The Assisi Compilation* reports Francis saying to a potential donor of land:

> 'When the brothers . . . find someone who wants to give them enough land to build a place, have a garden, and whatever is necessary for them, they must first consider how much land is enough for them, always considering the holy poverty we have promised, and the good example we are bound to offer to others.'. . . For this reason he did not want the brothers to have to be assigned to places in large groups, because it seemed to him that it was difficult to observe poverty fully.[27]

No doubt Francis had in his mind images of the grand Benedictine Abbeys he must have seen in his travels across Italy and into France with his merchant father. This was not the kind of life he aspired to now. When pressed to take on the Rule of St Benedict or the Constitutions of the Cistercians he simply replied that he wanted to be 'a new kind of fool'.[28] He was probably happiest in the early days of the order, when there were still only a few brothers. As more and more joined, he became progressively less able to cope with the administration of the burgeoning order and resigned his position of leadership first to Brother Peter of Catania and then to Brother Elias.[29] Large groups of religious unnerved him.

Although there were to be only a few brothers living together in the hermitages, still they would need to erect buildings of some form for shelter. Continuing with the account from the Assisi Compilation we see what Francis envisaged his hermitages would look like:

After receiving the bishop's blessing, let them go and have a big ditch dug around the land which they received for building the place, and as a sign of holy poverty and humility, let them place a hedge there, instead of a wall. Afterwards they may have poor little houses built, of mud and wood, and some little cells where the brothers can sometimes pray and where, for their own greater decency and also to avoid idle words, they can work.

They may also have churches made; however, the brothers must not have large churches made, in order to preach to the people there or for any other reason, for it is greater humility and better example when the brothers go to other churches to preach, so that they may observe holy poverty and their humility and decency.

And if prelates and clerics, religious or secular, should sometimes visit their places, their poor house, little cells, and churches in that place will preach to them and edify them.[30]

Reading this description, it is hard not to be reminded of the hermitage at Shepherds Law in Northumberland. From the hedge surrounding the compound to the successive 'little cells' established through the years in caravans and lean-to sheds, this has been a very Franciscan construction. The house may be built of stone rather than mud and wood, but even that mirrors the local building traditions and blends the building into the landscape. Of course, the church itself preaches to those who visit, not by its grandeur but by its unassuming and intricate beauty, where every detail has been planned and preceded by prayer. Even the number of cells, enough for no more than three or four brothers, mirrors the directions of the *Rule for Hermitages*.

One distinctive aspect of the *Rule for Hermitages* is the regulation that two of the brothers should act as 'mother' and the other one or two be a 'son'; together they live the life of the sisters of Bethany, Martha actively caring for the contemplative Mary sat at the feet of their friend Jesus. The Martha and Mary analogy was almost a commonplace in medieval religious literature, and Aelred of Rievaulx had already applied it to hermits in his *Rule of Life for a Recluse*, but the periodic exchange of roles was a new contribution by Francis. The use of the term 'mother' may reflect the much closer relationship Francis had with his own mother, as compared with the unresolved breakdown in relations with his father Pietro Bernadone. Equally it may arise from Francis's keen sense of the complementarity of male and female in God's creation, something he sang about in his Canticle of the Creatures, praising Brother Sun and Sister Moon, Brother Fire and Sister Water.[31] Above all this was a communal vision of a life of prayer and solitude; it was about being alone together. Mutual care was offered not just between the 'mothers' and 'sons', but in the form of the *custos* and minister who would visit the hermitage from time to time. Although some of the most famous of the early Franciscans, such as Brother Bernard and Brother Giles, seem to have lived much of their lives as solitaries,[32] the norm for Francis and his brothers was to maintain fraternal support by living together even as hermits. This early vision of mutuality in the hermitages seems to have been slightly lost in the later description of the Portiuncula examined above, where already the lay brothers are serving the clerical brothers as Martha to Mary, but this reflects an increasing tension within the whole order as it became progressively clericalized.

The question arises as to whether this stay in a hermitage was envisaged as a long-term or even permanent form of life, or just as a short period of retreat before returning to a more active form of mission. In a helpful footnote to the text of this Rule, Armstrong et al. point to the difficulties of translation here:

> *Stare* [to stay] is a difficult word to translate with accuracy since it has a sense of permanence as well as transience. Thus the practice of staying in hermitages may be interpreted in terms of a vocation in itself or of a period of recollection. *Religiose* [in a religious way] suggests monastic terminology which, in the twelfth century, speaks of *eremitica conversatio* or *rigor eremiticae conversationis* and called for a) physical distance from centres of urban activity; b) distinctive architecture keeping the 'world' at a distance and minimizing interaction among those within; and c) rules imposing and maintaining silence.[33]

In short, we do not know how long the friars would stay in one particular hermitage, but it makes sense to say that there must have been some stability in leading such a life. Even if some brothers came for a short period of time, others would surely have found this to be their primary vocation. Indeed, some clearly longed for a life in a hermitage, but were forbidden by Francis because of their existing pastoral responsibilities, as Francis says in his *Letter to a Minister (1221–1223)*:

> You must consider as grace all that impedes you from loving the Lord God and whoever has become an impediment to you, whether brothers or others, even if they lay hands on you . . . And love them in this and do not wish that they be better Christians. And let this be more than a hermitage for you.[34]

Life in a hermitage is not simply an escape from the troubles of the world. As the desert fathers and mothers often said, those who flee the cities for the desert bring their demons with them!

Continuing with the *Rule for Hermitages*, the brothers are expected to say or sing the daily office as all clerics were bound to do. Francis had a strong commitment to corporate prayer:

> He celebrated the canonical hours with no less awe than devotion. Although he was suffering from diseases of the eyes, stomach, spleen and liver, he did not want to lean against a wall or partition when he was chanting the psalms. He always fulfilled his hours standing up straight and without a hood, without letting his eyes wander and without dropping syllables.[35]

To encourage him in this practice he always wanted to have a cleric brother with him, so that between them they could recite the versicles and responses. Lay brothers, often illiterate, were expected only to recite a certain number of Paternosters (the Lord's Prayer) at the times of the canonical hours. For all, the day started with compline, the last prayers said before sleep; then the brothers would rise at midnight for the long readings of matins; shorter services would mark the progression of the day – prime at the first hour of the day, then terce at 9 a.m., sext at noon, none at 3 p.m. and finally vespers at sunset. It is unclear from the text how many of these services would have been said in common in the hermitages, and how many individually in the cell. At first there may have been no common chapel. But it is clear that prayer is in large measure the 'work' of the day. Prayer and sleep are the two activities allotted to the time in the cell, the apportioning of time between the two no doubt varying from friar to friar. Francis himself seems to have hardly slept at all. His practice of praying through the night was what most convinced his first companion, Bernard of Quintavalle, to renounce his wealth and join Francis in a life of prayer and penance.[36] Francis's practice of prayer was transformative in a way that he was barely able to hide:

> When he returned from his private prayers, in which he was changed almost into a different man, he tried his best to resemble the others; lest, if he appeared glowing, the breeze of favour might cancel what he had gained . . . Finally, his custom was to be so secret and quiet in rising for prayer [at night] that none of his companions would notice his rising or praying. But in the evening he made a good loud noise in going to bed, so that everyone would hear him as he went to rest.[37]

## A common meal

As well as praying, of course, the hermit brothers had to eat. Here the Rule states that the 'sons' may beg food from the 'mothers' after terce, for the love of God. This act reinforced their solidarity with each other, and with all the mendicant friars throughout the world. All were in some sense beggars at the table of the Lord, whether or not they went to beg from door to door, as Francis himself had done along with his companions in the early days of the order. Then the Rule states: 'And they may not permit anyone to enter or eat in the enclosure where they dwell.' This could be interpreted to mean that the 'sons' eat outside the enclosure with the 'mothers'.[38] But it seems to me more natural to take 'enclosure' to mean the hedge surrounding the whole site, so that 'anyone' in this sentence refers to people coming in from the outside. In this way, the enclosure of the whole hermitage is maintained, and strangers are not allowed to come and eat there, no doubt bringing with them the 'idle talk' of the news of the world. Having said this, it would perhaps have been unlikely that the friars would eat on their own in their cells, though this was the contemporary Carthusian model that Francis would have been familiar with from his visits to Italian Charterhouses. One story recorded by Celano incidentally confirms this:

Saint Francis usually passed the whole day in an isolated cell [at the hermitage at Greccio], returning to the brothers only when pressed by necessity to take some food. He did not leave it for dinner at the assigned time because his hunger for contemplation was even more consuming, and often completely overpowered him.[39]

Food for the soul was more important to Francis than food for the body. For those reading these accounts today, this may seem an impossibly austere way of life. How did the friars survive without descending into physical ill-health and mental turmoil? Maybe some did not survive – certainly Francis himself died at the relatively early age of around 44 years old. But for Francis and the early friars, life in the hermitages could be a source of joy. Celano tells the story of a Spanish cleric who comes to visit St Francis and describes for him the way of life of a hermitage of Lesser Brothers in Spain. Half take care of the chores, leaving the other half free for contemplation, all exchanging roles each week. Then:

One day, the table was set and a signal called those who were away. All the brothers came together except one, who was among those contemplating. They waited a while, and then went to his cell to call him to table, but he was being fed by the Lord at a more abundant table. For they saw him lying on his face on the ground, stretched out in the form of a cross, and showing no signs of life; not a breath or a motion. At his head and at his feet there flamed twin candelabra, which lit up the cell with a wonderful golden light. They left him in peace . . . suddenly the light disappeared and the brother returned to his human self. He got up at once, came to the table, and confessed his fault for being late. 'That's the kind of thing', said the Spaniard, 'that happens in our country.' Saint Francis could not restrain himself for joy; He suddenly rose up to give praise, as if his only glory was this: hearing good things about the brothers. He burst out from the depths of his heart: 'I give you thanks Lord, Sanctifier and Guide of the poor, you who have gladdened me with this report about the brothers! Bless those brothers, I beg you, with a most generous blessing, and sanctify with a special gift all those who make their profession fragrant through good example!'[40]

On another occasion, Francis spoke of the friars in the hermitages as the ones who were, by their prayers, more significant in the evangelistic mission of the order than those who devoted their time to study and preaching.

These brothers of mine are my knights of the round table, the brothers who hide in deserted and remote places, to devote themselves more diligently to prayer and meditation, weeping over their sins and those of others, whose holiness is known to God, and is sometimes ignored by the brothers and people. And when their souls will be presented to the Lord by the angels, the Lord will then reveal to them the fruit and reward of their labours, that is, the many souls saved by their prayers, saying to them, 'My sons, behold these souls have been saved by your prayers, and since you were faithful in little things, I will set you over many.'[41]

Having said all this, the hermitage tradition remained a peripheral way of life within the Franciscan Order. Hermits came to be identified as part of the 'spirituals' movement of friars, comprising brothers who felt alienated from the organizational structures of the order and dismayed at what they saw as a diminution of the rigours of poverty expected by Francis in his Rule and Testament. In subsequent centuries, the hermitages were often associated with reform movements, such as the 'Houses of Prayer' or 'Houses of Gathering' for Recollects or Observant friars.[42] The Capuchin Order of reformed Franciscans began as a hermitage or *ritiro* movement, emphasizing poverty and prayer. The Carmelite reform of Teresa of Avila was deeply influenced by the writings of Francisco de Osuna OFM and the Franciscan reformer Peter of Alcantara, both teaching recollection in prayer. Although never numerically ascendant in the order, it is arguable that the Franciscan hermits lived always at the heart of the order. Indeed, Francis could even say that, in a sense, all his brothers were truly hermits in as much as they were men of prayer:

Go, in the name of the Lord, two by two along the way, humbly and decently, in strict silence from dawn until terce, praying to the Lord in your hearts. And let no idle or useless words be mentioned among you. Although you are travelling, nevertheless, let your behaviour be as humble and as decent as if you were staying in a hermitage or a cell because wherever we are or wherever we travel, we always have a cell with us. Brother Body is our cell, and the soul is the hermit who remains inside the cell to pray to God and meditate on him.[43]

## Notes

1 See Rosalind B. Brooke, *The Image of St Francis: Responses to Sainthood in the Thirteenth Century*, Cambridge, Cambridge University Press, 2006, pp. 433ff.

2 R. W. Southern, *Western Society and the Church in the Middle Ages*, Harmondsworth, Penguin, 1970, p. 286.

3 Quoted in Dominic Monti, 'Franciscan Life and Urban Life', in Ken Himes OFM (ed.), *Franciscans in Urban Ministry*, St Bonaventure, NY, Franciscan Institute Publications, 2002, p. 6.

4 See Neslihan Şenocak, *The Poor and the Perfect: The Rise of Learning in the Franciscan Order, 1209–1310*, New York, Cornell University Press, 2012, for an account of the draw of the university towns for the early Franciscans.

5 See Thomas of Eccleston, *The Coming of the Franciscans*, trans. Leo Sherley-Price, London, Mowbray, 1964.

6 Southern, *Western Society*, p. 287.

7 C. H. Lawrence, *The Friars: The Impact of the Early Mendicant Movement on Western Society*, London, Longman, 1994, pp. 152ff.

8 Monti, 'Franciscan Life', p. 19.

9 See C. H. Lawrence, *Medieval Monasticism: Forms of Religious Life in Western Europe in the Middle Ages*, London, Longman, 1984, pp. 193–4.

10 Thomas of Celano, *The Remembrance of the Desire of a Soul (2 Cel.)* 58, in R. Armstrong, W. Hellmann and W. Short (eds), *Francis of Assisi: Early Documents, Volume 2, The Founder (FAED 2)*, New York, New City Press, 2000, p. 286.

11 Quoted in Lawrence, *The Friars*, p. 102.

12 *2 Cel.* 57, in *FAED 2*, p. 231.

13 The terms 'hermit' and 'solitary', though often confused, are not synonymous. The hermit is one who lives in deserted regions (Greek: *erymos*), whether alone or in small groups, often with disciples gathered around an elder or teacher in the ways of prayer.

14 From Thomas of Celano, *The Life of Saint Francis (1 Cel.)* 71, in R. Armstrong, W. Hellmann and W. Short (eds), *Francis of Assisi: Early*

*Documents, Volume 1, The Saint* (*FAED* 1), New York, New City Press, 1999, p. 244.

15 *1 Cel.* 6, in *FAED* 1, pp. 187–8.

16 *Assisi Compilation* 54, in *FAED* 2, p. 152.

17 *The Legend of Three Companions* 25, in *FAED* 2, p. 84.

18 *Legend of the Three Companions* 36, in *FAED* 2, p. 89.

19 *The Beginning of A Mirror of Perfection of the Status of a Lesser Brother*, trans. Paul Sabatier, in R. Armstrong, W. Hellmann and W. Short (eds), *Francis of Assisi: Early Documents, Volume 3, The Prophet* (*FAED* 3), New York, New City Press, 2001, pp. 299–300. This is admittedly a late text (*c.*1318), but may well enshrine traditions going back to Brother Leo, a close companion of Francis (see *Mirror of Perfection*, pp. 209–10). Much the same material is also found in the earlier *Assisi Compilation* 56.

20 *Mirror of Perfection, FAED* 3, p. 300.

21 One such example can be found at *Assisi Compilation* 74 (*FAED* 2, p. 177): 'Blessed Francis found the hermitage of the brothers at Greccio to be becoming and poor and the inhabitants, although poor and simple, were more pleasing to him than those of the rest of the region. For this reason he rested and stayed there, especially because there was a very poor cell, very isolated, in which the holy father would stay.'

22 After 1217, as this was when the office of minister was first introduced and before 1222, because by then the friars were allowed oratories and celebrations of the Mass, of which there is no mention in the Rule.

23 *FAED* 1, pp. 61–2.

24 See in particular André Cirino and Josef Raischl (eds), *Franciscan Solitude*, St Bonaventure, NY, The Franciscan Institute, 1995, for an excellent set of essays on the Franciscan eremitical tradition in general and the interpretation of the *Rule for Hermitages* by Francis of Assisi in particular.

25 *2 Cel.* 71, *FAED* 2, p. 295.

26 This conception of the role of religious is strikingly similar to that of Buddhist monks and nuns, the *sangha* (monastic community) being seen as a 'field of merit', a suitable object of the generosity of the laity.

27 *Assisi Compilation* 58, *FAED* 2, p. 160.

28 *Assisi Compilation* 18, *FAED* 2, p. 132.

29 See Andre Vauchez, *Francis of Assisi: The Life and Afterlife of a Medieval Saint*, New Haven, CT, Yale University Press, 2012, pp. 110–17 and 122–7 for a critical analysis of Francis' leadership skills.

30 *FAED* 2, p. 161.

31 *FAED* 1, pp. 113–14.

32 Celano bewails the loss of fervour in the Franciscan hermitages in his own day (the generation after Francis): 'We know that the fathers who went before us stood out as solitary flowers. May the hermits of our times not fall away from that earliest beauty!' (*2 Cel.* 179, *FAED* 2, p. 362).

33 *FAED* 1, p. 61.

34 *FAED* 1, p. 97.

35  2 *Cel.* 96, *FAED* 2, p. 311.

36  *Deeds of the Blessed Francis and his Companions* 1, *FAED* 3, p. 435.

37  2 *Cel.* 99, *FAED* 2, pp. 312–13.

38  See Jean François Godet-Calogeras, '*Illi qui volunt religiose stare in eremis*: Eremetical Practice in the Life of the Early Franciscans', in Timothy J. Johnson (ed.), *Franciscans at Prayer*, The Medieval Franciscans Vol. 4, Leiden, Brill, 2007, pp. 307–32 (328).

39  2 *Cel.* 45, *FAED* 2, p. 277.

40  2 *Cel.* 178, *FAED* 2, p. 361.

41  *Assisi Compilation* 103, *FAED* 2, p. 208.

42  See Cirino and Raischl, *Franciscan Solitude*, for further details of these movements; also Ronald M. Mrozinski OFM Conv., *Franciscan Prayer Life: The Franciscan-Contemplative Synthesis and the Role of Centers of Prayer*, Chicago, Franciscan Herald Press, 1981.

43  *Mirror of Perfection*, *FAED* 3, p. 309.

# 7

# The Monastic Sacrament in Life, Liturgy, Saints and Buildings

## GEORGE GUIVER

## Monastic life

Monastic life is a culture of its own, a rich context not easily understood from outside. For new recruits, it takes a good while to get under the skin of this way of life inclined at an angle to what is familiar. This book began with its deepest sources and has gone on to examine some of the historical and geographical contexts that are there in the tacit awareness of any religious community. Taking Shepherds Law as our example, that gives us, among other things, Northumbrian monasticism in the time of Bede, the monastic strands in Anglicanism and the wider ecumenical context, in which the ancient churches play a major part. Shepherds Law perhaps approximates best to the Eastern skete, and this has emerged more through a process of realization than as a conscious aim. These strands lead us through the door into a particular world of perception, in which a 'sense of the Church' is coloured in and given tangible form in the shape of monasticism's historical heritage – in other words, as a Samoan or a Laplander might say of their culture: 'this is who we are'.

We need at this point to delve further into the issue of tacit awareness, and for this a simple story can start us off. I was praying at the back of a hospital chapel when a man came in, walked up to the altar and put his hand on it, held it there for quite a long time and then went away. Perhaps he had come from holding the hand of someone he loved: now he came to hold God's hand (or ask God to hold his). Holding the hand of an ill relative can in charged circumstances be a necessary act, something inevitable and beyond words. Here, for this man, it had seemed natural to do the same with God.

In Western Christianity, since the Renaissance and the Enlightenment, such a physical approach to prayer has given place to more abstract understandings. The Reformation pruned back sharply the physical side of Christian practice, and then the eighteenth-century Enlightenment in the Continental Roman Catholic Church followed in its steps by attempting in various areas of Europe to do likewise, scorning as superstitious things that were on the same level as putting a hand on an altar.[1] Humanity's true mode of discourse with God was now thought to be primarily cerebral. It is at home with words, not things and actions, and its affective content is individual ('personal') and internal.

In more recent years, this has all begun to be rolled back again. Purely cerebral worship is no longer satisfactory, if ever it was, and we have been witnessing a returning march of full and frequent participation in the Eucharist, a new appreciation of the other sacraments and sacramentals, and a cornucopia of inventiveness in praying in physical ways; we need only think of Christingle, the great popularity of votive candles or the practices that find their way into contemporary 'imaginative' worship, not to mention the phenomenon of charismatic worship. Many now delight in celebrating the rich practices of Holy Week, the growing employment of the arts and increasing interest in devising worship rich in symbols and symbolic actions. The widely popular giving of the peace (only unpopular where its theological meaning and ancient pedigree are not understood) compares well with holding a relation's hand when they are ill or putting your hand on the altar.

Still lurking in the background in all of us, however, are old attitudes which come out in a need to see some immediate results from our symbolic actions. If the Eucharist doesn't leave us feeling assured and strengthened, we may tire of it. On the whole, we have not yet relearnt in religion what we take for granted in other walks of life: that symbolic actions can work their work simply by being done. You don't need to feel anything as you shout goodbye going out of the front door. You don't need to feel you have 'got something out of it' when you sit by the fire with your spouse. So we need yet to learn to rest confident in God's promises when we address God, without needing to have some kind of experience. The need to 'get something out of it' reveals a weakness in our stance of faith, which could be described as being stuck in a constant state of courtship without ever having covenanted ourselves. One truth the hospital chapel story reveals, however, is that *need*, a dependence on help or support from somewhere, increases the willingness to believe. It is likely that the man was in need, such unidentifiable need as we feel when we are at a loss, and he simply decided he wanted to lay his hand on the altar, he did it and that was that. It was now part of the fabric of that day for him, and perhaps a part of the fabric of every day for him for that period. We can be most powerfully alive when we are in need, something that is a theme of the Christian gospel, where God is more likely to meet us in our weakness than in our strength. Our current needs today are driving us back to rediscover and expand the physical side of our relating with God, and here we need to beware of the quest for experience. This is because the most enduring payback in relating to God (as to our spouse or friends) is in the long term. You see the fruits sometimes after years, and they only come with faithfulness and trust that are not dependent on experience.

We would expect monastic life to be a deeply spiritual life, concerned with inward journeying towards God, in quiet and internal reflection. That is true – it is those things – silence, prayer, solitude and a certain kind of peace. In order for them to be possible, however, there has to be hard work, a busy day and much engagement with physical reality – putting-the-hand-on-the-altar writ large. The interior journey is closely bound up with pouring energy into numerous daily services, study, silent prayer, cooking, cleaning, finance, maintenance and other practical tasks in the running of a sizeable establishment, committee meetings, dealing with services and suppliers, looking after guests and responding to a manifold variety of things that crop up each day. St Benedict in his Rule for Monks links this with the altar. The monks are told to treat the ordinary implements of daily work as if they were the vessels of the altar.[2] God is known in the doing of the work, and Christ is present, not least in the guests who come. Private prayer, surprisingly, hardly gets into Benedict's picture, while for him God is perpetually encountered and known is in the daily services and daily work – in other words, in the sheer running of the place. For St Benedict, this notion of the life of the place is highlighted as a central feature of monastic life – so much so as to be the subject of one of the three monastic vows: *conversatio morum*, a vow to give oneself to this way of life and its inherited wisdom.

## The monastic sacrament

We cannot understand monastic life without taking account of the fact that Christianity uses physical things and actions, just as normal human beings do in their daily lives – we give presents, we shake hands or embrace to express things that words are not enough to say, we find it important to decorate our houses, to perform ceremonies like those of Remembrance Sunday and so on. It is not by chance that in all religions spiritual realities need to be expressed in physical ways. In Christianity, this principle has been taken the whole hog. In order to save us from all the difficulties we are in – whether it is our deep imperfections and their sad effects, or our fears, especially of death, or our difficulty in believing in God, or any of the other things which weigh upon us – God brought himself to come among us, to become one of us and share our situation, in Jesus, God-with-us as a living, physical person. This is the principle of the incarnation, a principle without which Christianity cannot possibly be understood, and nor can Christian monasticism.

Sacraments connect the earthly with the heavenly. So in baptism a new Christian is (or ought to be[3]) plunged into water, in Holy Communion we receive Jesus in bread and wine, those who are sick have hands laid upon them and are anointed with oil[4] – three ways in which God breaks all barriers to come directly to us, physically. These things are called sacraments, and there are many more, all of them coming to us from the most fundamental sacrament of all, which is the Church.[5]

Before the High Middle Ages, when thinking about sacraments became unhelpfully narrowed, life under monastic vows was often referred to as a sacrament. More recent thinking has come to show that the medieval division of Christian practices into sacraments (just seven) and a lesser order of practices called 'sacramentals' (such as blessings, or candles, or ashes on Ash Wednesday) is misleading. Starting from the premise that the Church is the foundational sacrament, it follows that all of its life partakes in some way of the sacramental dimension.

If the life of every religious community of whatever type is seen as sacrament, then two things follow: (1) It is a life rooted in the dispensation ushered in by the incarnation of Jesus – it is one of the ways in which the gospel is incarnated; (2) It will be a focused bringing together of the everyday and the supernatural: all its physical aspects, whether people or things or activities, will be seen as material of the sacrament, as the bread and wine are in the eucharistic offering and the receiving of Communion. Every aspect of this way of life, whether easy or difficult, joyful or painful, will be seen positively as a place of encounter with Christ, who is incarnate in all of it. This being so, it will be helpful to examine a little more closely some practical aspects of the life of religious communities.

## Worship

Monastic life is not simply a going-apart to pursue an interior journey – it is first of all an exterior journey of physical activities and relationships. The best way to understand this is to begin with worship. A common and laudable approach to worship in many a parish church is to aim to put on a good show, with fine vestments and music, good participation and a sense of family. Another parish church might put on a lively show with worship songs accompanied by a group, while a cathedral will aim for classical excellence and worship that will stir the heart. All of these use such resources partly to have an *effect* on the worshippers and catch them up in a movement of all the participants towards the divine. Such forms of worship are a response to God's call to worship God in precisely such a way. For all their necessity and excellence, however, they do hide a danger: they can skate uneasily between helping people to relate to God and hindering that by drawing attention to the human element; in Christian worship, there will always be a risk of seeking to engineer effects, producing a picture of God that comes from us, when we need a picture that comes from God. This aim to have an effect is necessary but always risky not far below the surface.

## Mission and covenant

We can think of two poles: mission and covenant. Mission-worship seeks to win people over and to attract. This however is only a transitional stage on the way to the further stage of covenant, when we have been won over, we have a more mature acceptance of the Christian faith and are ready for more solid food, rather than milk. Worship characterized by covenant cannot always guarantee to be pleasurable, attractive or heart-stirring. Like family life or our daily job, there are frequent occasions when we do it simply because it is there and we are committed to it. This is worship understood as work. All worship needs a dash of 'mission' in it, even in a monastery, as there is always need for a little help and encouragement here and there, but we don't get discouraged if we don't find that, because we now know that the most lasting fruits come over the long term. In this case, we are simply content to get on with it as the daily bread and butter of the relationship with the God we love and who loves us.

Back in 1985 Neil Postman, in his book *Amusing Ourselves to Death*, saw that in our society entertainment was becoming a psychological need for people, replacing more serious and mature ways of reflecting and gaining insight.[6] Since then, this has been taken further by the Internet and social media, so that increasing numbers of us habitually flit between unrelated snippets of information and 'fun', and are less and less capable of sustained and focused development of our knowledge and understanding. In church, this atmosphere of entertainment can give us the priest who behaves like a compère or chat-show host, heavy reliance on light music with light words and the enthroning of what is 'exciting' or 'lively'. Needless to say, these have their place, not least in the mission to bring people in – for people who are likely to be brought in by that way of worshipping, at any rate. There is, however, a trajectory to be followed, from milk to solid food, from mission to covenant. It is to the dimension of covenant that religious communities particularly witness, where worship is happily embraced as a commitment and can sometimes feel more like work than fun, not so much uplifting us as taking us down into depths, where we grow in knowledge of ourselves, of others and of God – in other words, taking us towards reality rather than illusion. Worship needs to keep these two things, mission and covenant, in the right balance – we all need a bit of mission to help us persevere, but there is a deeper flourishing that can only come at the level of covenant.

## Simplicity

In a religious community, there is the opportunity to reduce the risks here, and this is sought by a principle of simplicity. The simplicity to which members of religious communities are vowed affects their material goods, their way of life and its forms of work and recreation, their freedoms and their worship. Worship is done with care, and commands as much attention and imagination as in any parish church or cathedral, but the approach minimizes the risk of distraction into such things as a pursuit of experience or a 'feel-good effect', a pursuit of beauty or fun that can distract and divert us towards merely human goals or experience; the monastic approach minimizes the risk (though it can never banish it) of the temptation to pride (in our own achievements, or pride in the parish or cathedral, say, as an institution) and of self-consciousness ('Isn't this marvellous?'), and seeks to lessen the possibility of distraction from the quest for full engagement with the unadorned truth. This particular way of religious communities (or most of them) is a complementary way, not a more perfect one. In the parish, hearts have to be won and re-won by the worship, but monastic worship does not need that. Hearts are being won in other ways.

If the worship of religious communities tends to be simple, monastic simplicity should not mean philistinism. The nature of worship is that it will be offered with care and an eye for beauty, but in this case it will resonate with the monastic quest for humility and a commitment to simplicity of life. The worship will reflect the life and not be a departure from it. Simplicity speaks for itself and is in its own way sacramental: by reducing the plethora of things that can stitch us to earth, it enables a freedom for us to be stitched to heaven. It acts out in worship a reduced dependence on possessions and on a sense of our own importance and position in life (religious communities tend to delight in self-send-up). Life is not to be spurned – it is to be enjoyed, but simply. There is here a tacit sacramental sense that God is to be met in simplicity.

## Gratuitousness

Allied to this absence of a need to be won over is a sense of the givenness of worship. For a religious community, a 'sense of the Church' is always implicit, and together with it a sense of the *gratuitousness* of the offering – it is simply given without any sense of it being necessary to receive anything in return. The community knows, however, that in a way that might be quite unseen, it is receiving and contributing in one breath within a wondrous exchange, as the worship feeds into the hidden 'economy' of God. When people say to communities 'I'm glad you're there', the speakers have a sense of this. Somehow the religious community's worship is *contributing* and doing it on behalf of everybody. There are points where this breaks through: the Psalms in their constant returning to lament and grieving give voice to the world's voiceless, as the community utters their cries to God. Communities also receive many requests for intercession, as people perceive religious sisters and brothers to be, in the words of Walter Frere, 'God's remembrancers'. St Benedict puts his finger on the fact that you cannot measure or weigh up this process, when throughout his Rule he calls the daily offices *opus Dei*, the 'work of God'. It is work, simply there to be done, without thought for feelings or experiences or results – it is of inestimable worth simply in itself, and in the simple doing of it its work is done, in a way that can feel very objective: somehow in the actual objectiveness of it the religious sister or brother grows over the years to know that it is a sacrament, an outward and visible sign through which grace does its work.

Here is a key to helping people to pray today – giving yourself to an agreed round of prayer which is not just yours; it is the Church at prayer and you simply get on with it, like the Anglicans who used to say daily the Sunday collect.[7]

## Meals

Just as decision-making in chapter meetings shares something in common with the worship in the church, so does the refectory. It is important that a community have meals together, even if this is not always easy in communities that have an active ministry. The table has a place in the daily round, and the meals have something of the character of the liturgy. They tend to be ritualized and to be as non-negotiable as the community's worship – I am committed to being there at every meal, even if there may be times when I have no appetite. There is a link between the tables of refectory and altar, both belonging together in the day's sacramental activities.

## Buildings

The buildings have a key role in enabling the life to work. A central concept is that of holding a place, a piece of ground, where a way of life can be established according to norms different from those in the world around it. In the process, this piece of ground generates a climate all of its own. The building of first importance is the church or chapel. In the Western tradition as it developed in the Middle Ages, the choir-stalls came to be a significant presence in the church, saying something to everyone who enters, as well as to their users, about what is central in this way of life – the daily sitting under the Word, all together. The church is the key to the monastic site – daily prayer is what the community is there for, and a stable place of worship is necessary to a stable frame of mind for doing the work; and so considerable resources need to go into providing an eloquent place for this. A religious community's church or chapel functions as a concentration of the sacramental nature of the whole life and its location and buildings. Stephen Platten has spoken elsewhere of this sacramental nature of church buildings.[8] There are religious communities where buildings tend to be minimal or functional, and that can go with a deliberate choice for minimalism (as with the Cistercian reform) or with a more 'apostolic' form of life and ministry, where the God-centred dialogue is located more within the daily secular world around them; but for most forms of monastic life the aspiration is different, something examined more fully in our later chapter on buildings.

If we are using the word 'sacrament' in the broad way I have described, the monastic lands and buildings are then seen as sacramental of the life: at the same time as needing to be more extensive and spacious than the individual occupants would elsewhere need, they will reflect the simplicity of the community's calling, while also being a gracious and pleasing offering to God, rather than merely functional (although there are communities whose commitment to simplicity has led them to opt for that). Every way of life is influenced by its environment and is in dialogue with it, and the monastic community is perpetually in dialogue with its buildings and land and the people it shares them with, with an understanding that God will be encountered in this relationship.

## Hospitality and service

Our imaginary tree's roots are in the air, but its leaves on the ground. The internal life of a religious community overflows in a variety of ways into the world around it, and here hospitality has always been important: guests coming to stay for a few days or a longer period of retreat, and individuals and groups of many kinds, including the many who may come to a monastery perhaps just for the inside of a day. A monastic guesthouse in the charge of a member of the community is one of the standard requirements for a monastery of any size. In addition, in the times before public health services, communities were places where the sick and needy could expect assistance. This was a major concern in Britain at the time of the sixteenth-century dissolution of the monasteries, an anxiety that proved fully justified as this free and generous service simply disappeared.

Communities are also inevitably involved, even if in limited ways, in the social and economic life of the place in which they are set. In medieval England, this could get out of hand, as in the terrible relationship between the monks of St Edmundsbury and the townsfolk. At Norwich in 1272 the townspeople entered and set fire to the cathedral, an event that led to the rebuilding of the cloister over the next 150 years. One of the reasons for constant cycles of reform in monastic history has been the tendency of monasteries to be successful economic units, containing numbers of able people doing productive work without being paid and also receiving financial support from donations.

St Francis in the twelfth century attempted to break out of this, leading the life out on to the streets to be at the service of the people. That was the beginning of a mushrooming of orders nowadays called 'apostolic', groups of people living under vows, often in the midst of ordinary life, engaged in such ministries as nursing, teaching, helping the needy. British television viewers will know something of this from the popular series *Call the Midwife*.[9] This can be a way of life very different from that of a monastery, but the principles are the same: a life centred and rooted in God, in the context of a community, and of vows that embrace a high degree of self-renunciation. There are communities that fall somewhere in the middle, but the two ways of life, 'monastic' and 'apostolic', are distinctive – apostolic orders live for their pastoral ministry, while monastic communities are called to be a kind of spiritual storage-heater, a place where the spiritual life is concentrated and stored up, and then radiates to the many people who come into the climate it generates.

## Climate

Jesus collected around him a group of close followers, the Twelve. He sought to cultivate among them, within their small circle, a different way of thinking and being. The special climate that grew up among them began to open their eyes and change them. Gradually seeing with different eyes, they started to develop new powers of intuition, new ways of seeing the world, a new way of being human beings: imperfect, certainly, but it is clear that in Jesus they encountered something that left them changed for ever. They could not always live it well, any more than an art student might paint a perfect portrait, but their apprehension of it was strong and enduring.

We can see this climate in the group as a microclimate, the climate of Jesus-with-his-people. Microclimates are small areas where special conditions prevail, enabling a particular kind of flora and fauna to flourish. An example could be the inside wall of a well where ferns might grow that are not otherwise found in that region. A very different microclimate would be the contained conditions of a nuclear reactor. The microclimate of life with Jesus in the small group of the Disciples was a living reality, and since then it has been passed down through the centuries as the climate of the Church. The Church has always operated on the principle of the microclimate. It is as small and vulnerable as the ferns on the inside of a well, but also akin to a nuclear reactor – it is God's special instrument for carrying his mighty works to their full effect. The Church, the people of God, is an *environment* that enables the release of powerful forces that are normally repressed. This environment can be seen as a culture filled with life by the Holy Spirit and passed on through every generation since Christ first nurtured it among his Disciples. Within the microclimate of the Church, religious communities are perhaps an intensification of the same thing, and in some ways a microclimate within the microclimate.

How may the parish be an effective microclimate of this kind? The story of Jesus and the community he nurtured into being would suggest that, yes, somehow the parish is called to embody the climate of Jesus and to be a milieu where those who enter find their presuppositions and notions of plausibility beginning to crack, or perhaps heal. Those who come seeking will be surprised by something other than they were looking for. Then they will find themselves entering upon a conversion process, as their conception of what is 'normal' begins to be subverted and changed. Such a climate will only exist where the established members are themselves going through the same process of conversion day by day. The microclimate affects both those within it and those who encounter it from outside. It is sacramental: there is a limit to what can be planned or devised, for we are dealing with something that is a fruit of life in the Holy Spirit. The desire is not to generate this climate, but to love God and the things of God with our whole being, and the rest follows, for the parish itself is of the nature of a sacrament.

This chapter has tried to sketch out something of the sacramental nature of monastic life, while showing that this principle applies to the whole Church, and every community and parish within it. Two elements of this, buildings and music, are so significant that they now need further exploration in chapters of their own.

## Notes

1 On this surprising blip in the history of the Roman Catholic Church, see George Guiver, *Vision Upon Vision: Processes of Change and Renewal in Christian Worship*, Norwich, Canterbury Press, 2009, Chapter 8.

2 Rule of St Benedict 31.10.

3 Total immersion in baptism is presumed by the New Testament, and was the norm until recent centuries. Even the Book of Common Prayer of 1662 presumes it – the rubric says that the priest 'shall dip it [the child] in the water warily and discreetly'.

4 On anointing of the sick, see Mark 6.13, James 5.14 and, for modern practice, Canon B37.3 of the Canons of the Church of England.

5 See, for example, E. Schillebeeckx, *Church: The Human Story of God*, London, SCM Press, 1990; also Rowan Williams, 'The Church as Sacrament', *International Journal for the Study of the Christian Church* 10, no. 1 (February 2010), pp. 6–12.

6 N. Postman, *Amusing Ourselves to Death: Public Discourse in an Age of Show Business*, Harmondsworth, Penguin, revised, 2005.

7 See also G. Guiver, *Everyday God*, London, SPCK, 1994 (and Mirfield Publications, 2016).

8 Stephen Platten, 'Building Sacraments', *Theology* 117, no. 2 (March/April 2014), pp. 83–93.

9 *Call the Midwife* has been a highly successful television series created by Heidi Thomas, depicting the cooperation of the Anglican Community of the Nursing Sisters of St John the Divine and local midwives in the East End of London in the 1940s and 1950s.

# 8

# Gregorian Chant and Monastic Life

## DOM XAVIER PERRIN OSB

### Introduction: From Ely to Shepherds Law

It was as he attended evensong in Ely Cathedral one evening in the 1950s that Brother Harold received a sort of revelation of the world of Gregorian chant. He would say later: 'It was a seminal experience.' On his way to Shepherds Law, he was to meet many times again with the chant. One of these occasions was his years spent at Glasshampton – 1957–62 and 1969–70. 'The novice master', he writes in the account of his journey, 'inspired in me his love of the Gregorian tradition of plainsong for the daily services.'[1] The books and the spiritual presence of Father William Sirr were also around. The latter had been very much part of a movement of rediscovery of the chant in the Anglican Church. It happened at a time when there was in the Roman Catholic Church an impressive revival of Gregorian chant following the work of the monks of Solesmes and under the guidance of the popes. Chant, translated and adapted from Latin to English, was indeed a feature of the religious renewal in the Anglo-Catholic movement. In the same context, at Mirfield, Walter Frere's interest in the chant led him to publish his famous books on the Sarum Rite and also to shape the liturgy of the Community of the Resurrection with an English version of chant at its heart. Through an Anglicized version of Gregorian chant, one got the feeling of reconnecting with the tradition of prayer of the Church.

When Brother Harold arrived at his hermitage in 1970, he began the long work of composing a liturgy adapted to the needs of the new community he had in mind. It was obviously to be in English and chant was the evident choice. Evident, but not easy, as he soon felt the need to give it as much as possible of the supple and living harmony between text and melody which is the very characteristic of Gregorian chant. He had experienced it during his frequent visits to the Solesmes Benedictine monks of Quarr Abbey on the Isle of Wight. There he had conversations with the famous choir master Dom Jean Hébert Desroquettes. This background helped him, though not a fully trained musician himself, to feel confident enough to begin correcting and editing already translated antiphons and hymns as well as creating his own adaptations of other pieces. He gathered a corpus of English antiphons in chant for the whole liturgical cycle mainly from the Sarum and Solesmes books – including the most recent editions of the antiphonary (2005). This is still a work in progress to a certain extent. Additions or corrections continue to bring this unique antiphonary to its completion and perfection.

Chant must therefore be considered an important feature of Brother Harold's monastic vision. The hermit's liturgical prayer is not a silent breviary but a sung antiphonary. Even alone, the monk sings the divine office. Chant is part of the fullness of his life and witness. It is one of the elements which gives the liturgy at Shepherds Law its ecclesial fullness. Indeed, according to Brother Harold, chant relates most especially to the catholicity of the Church, to the mystery of communion in love which lies at the heart of the Church's identity. After reviewing the main forms of the chant, this chapter will attempt to formulate some aspects of the theology of the chant and to describe the spiritual experience it makes possible.

## Forms
### Psalmody

In the beginning is the Word of God and, most especially, the words of the Psalms. Psalmody is the mother of chant. Most chant is either *for* psalmody, as with the antiphons which precede and follow the recitation of the psalms and canticles we find in the antiphonary, or *from* psalmody, as with the elaborated pieces of the graduale which are sung at Mass. This link cannot be sufficiently stressed. It is from psalmody that chant receives its main features.

The peaceful and powerful recitation of the words of the Psalms has been the substance of the Church's prayer throughout the ages. Sung psalmody is first of all about a correct and good pronunciation of the words within the verse. The verse – composed of two parts visibly separated, but indeed physiologically united by a breath – is the basic unity of signification and prayer. From the very beginning, chant is a concentrated act of singing and breathing which allows the most correct and full enunciation of the text possible. *Bene dicere* (saying well) and *bene cantare* (singing well) go together.

Music acts as a servant of the text, which always keeps pride of place. The melodies are not here in order to provide an ornament which would try to add some beauty to the verbal expression of concepts, as it were from outside. They are a fruit of the life, the beauty and indeed the power of the words of the Psalms. Music underlines this power. Melody serves it. The musical setting of the text expresses something of the fullness of the words and, at the same time, suggests something of the ineffable reality that lies beyond the words and towards which the words point. Music manifests the orientation of the words towards the mystery of the Word itself.

Even in the minimalist forms of the recto-tono (when the text is purely recited on one single note) or in the simplest types of psalmody, music invests the text with the power of harmony. The *cantus obscurior* of the words which fascinated Cicero[2] is put into full light by the support of the singing voice. Therefore the choice of a poetic translation of the Psalms is of foremost importance. It is not enough to render correctly the meaning of the sentences of the old Jewish prayers. One really wants a translation that, by the arrangement of the sounds and the stresses, gives access to the musical dimension of the text itself. In the Septuagint, the *psalterion* gave its name to the *psalms* which are prayers destined to be sung and accompanied with musical instruments because they are poetically composed. The Psalms belong to poetry and call for the harmonies of music.

### Antiphon

The short antiphons that accompany the psalms, or the more developed ones that introduce and conclude the recitation of the gospel canticles, introduce a new dimension of dialogue.

When the text of the antiphon is taken from the psalm, we could speak of a dialogue of the psalm with itself. The antiphon gives a direction. It highlights a verse or a few words. It acts as a revelation and an invitation. Exactly as the series of words which the antiphon sings, the whole text is virtually capable of being sung in a fuller and more developed mode than simple psalmody. The antiphon reminds us of the possibilities of the text – both musical and spiritual. There lies – it seems to say – a richness of music, truth and beauty. Even in the sober act of psalmody, a whole musical world is virtually present. This is not the time to explain it (as would be possible in the more elaborated pieces of the graduale). It is enough to suggest, to remind and – to tell the truth – it is enough for the loving soul to receive the delicate and subtle suggestion of the antiphon to be lifted up in a state of chant.

At other times, the antiphon will come from the prophets (for instance in Advent) or from the life of the saints (on their feast day). The psalm dialogues with other parts of Scripture and/or with the life of the Church at its highest degree of holiness. One could speak here of the *polyphony* of the word in the Church. There are many voices in the one voice of the Scriptures and in the one voice of the Church. These voices, though, sing in unison. They proclaim the one mystery of the one faith. To the spouse, everything speaks of her Bridegroom.

With the Gospel canticles – the Benedictus at lauds and the Magnificat at vespers – the antiphon can, on ferial days, be taken from the canticle. On Saturdays at vespers, it dialogues with the cycle of Scripture readings for vigils, which covers both the Old and the New Testaments. On Sundays, the antiphons for Benedictus and Magnificat normally come from the Gospel of the day. On the festival of the saints, they are often borrowed from the life of the saint. Advent, Christmastide, Lent and Eastertide offer a special antiphon for each morning and evening office. The Church sings the whole of Scripture, but especially the gospel – Matthew and John above all. She sings with Christ's words. She answers Christ's voice with the words of Christ. She honours Christ's presence.

Through the antiphons, what psalmody could have of the atemporal is connected with the *Hodie* – the liturgical 'Today' – of Christ's presence in the Church. The mystery enfolds in the time both as history and as presence. Liturgy honours history by the memory of the words and actions of Christ and the saint, but it mainly celebrates the presence. This is the way the Church opens the present world to the presence of the kingdom in its very midst (Luke 17.21). There lies the eschatological beauty of chant in which and through which the eternal liturgy has already begun.

## Responsory

Whereas the antiphon is immersed, as it were, in the stream of psalmody, the responsory is more static. A verse of the Psalms or another biblical text is singled out and sung, first by a soloist, then by the assembly (the hermit playing both roles, as it were). During psalmody, the dialogue is between the two choirs who unite to sing together the antiphon. In the responsory, the dialogue is between a soloist – the cantor – and the whole choir. The verse is sung by the cantor and repeated by all. The soloist then adds a second verse to which the choir answers by the repetition of the first verse (or of its final part). A doxology (Glory be) is often added as a third verse by the soloist, the choir answering again with the first verse. The melody follows a fixed pattern and remains very sober, though it can be more ornate on feasts.

Here the most important feature is repetition. The same few words are sung once by the soloist and three times by all. After the constant movement of psalmody and the pure listening to the reading of the Word of God in the short reading, the responsory is an answer to the word which focuses on one verse. This is chosen to evoke the mystery of either the hour, the day or the season. The purity of the intervals, the *sostenuto* of the voice, the clarity of the text make of it a very powerful statement through which the direction of prayer is expressed and reinforced.

## Hymn

There is a place in chant for Christian poetic meditation on the mysteries too. The hymn that opens each hour is a strophic poem composed on a fixed pattern of four (or six) verses which receive the same melody. There is a set of hymns for the ferial days. On diverse degrees of feast days, either the same text has a different music (as in the little hours of terce, sext and none, and compline) or, in the other hours, a new text with a proper melody is used, either for a season, or for a category of saints, or simply for this day only.

The rhythm does not have the same freedom and subtlety as in the other genres, as the music tends to be more loosely bonded with the text and can sometimes impose a measured rhythm on the text. The melodies, though, are usually composed in the same modal frame which comes from psalmody. The general mood of the chant is, however, kept on a slightly less profound level of contemplation.

## Litanies

Very close to psalmody by their musical genre, the litanies which conclude the offices concentrate and focus the prayer on a simple chord. Their mood is one of supplication. They express the movement of prayer which persists in supplication and which sums its request up so as to make it more efficacious. The Kyrie, the Our Father and the collect are part of these final prayers, all united by the same mood of intense and sober prayer.

## Graduale

The great pieces of the ordinary and the proper of the Mass in the graduale trace their origin to the different liturgical genres we have explored. Introits, communions and alleluias are ornamented antiphons. Graduals and offertories are developed responsories. The Kyrie and Agnus Dei are solemn litanies. The Gloria, Sanctus and Credo have similarities with the hymns.

Here the dialogue is between the pieces of chant and the readings of the day, or the mystery of the season or of the day. At the same time, the eucharistic orientation of the chant, implicit during the hours of the office, becomes explicit. Chant makes explicit the preparation of the soul for receiving the gift of the Presence at its highest level.

## A theology of the word
### Music and words

From the practice of, esteem for and love of the Psalms, the chant inherited a tremendous respect for the words. Ultimately, music comes from the words. The words and the phrase have a potential musicality which the chant enacts and reveals. What is this music of the words? It is more than the interplay of the phonemes. The sound and the movement of the words are part of the divine harmony which permeates the created world. In his address to representatives of the world of culture at Paris in 2012, Pope Benedict XVI spoke at length of this reality:

... the culture of singing is also the culture of being, and [that] the monks have to pray and sing in a manner commensurate with the grandeur of the word handed down to them, with its claim on true beauty. This intrinsic requirement of speaking with God and singing of him with words he himself has given, is what gave rise to the great tradition of Western music. It was not a form of private 'creativity', in which the individual leaves a memorial to himself and makes self-representation his essential criterion. Rather it is about vigilantly recognizing with the 'ears of the heart' the inner laws of the music of creation, the archetypes of music that the Creator built into his world and into men, and thus discovering music that is worthy of God, and at the same time truly worthy of man, music whose worthiness resounds in purity.[3]

Words without music would remain hidden and unfulfilled. Music without words could be in danger of enclosing itself in the world – hence the reservations of some fathers, including Augustine, as to the liturgical use of music. Words and music, that is chant, when 'purely' sung, give the fullest expression to man's answer to God's Word with the words of God.

### The voice in the cosmos: the modes
In a very simple way, the words sung on a single note, as in psalmody or any cantillation, are endowed with powerful cosmic resonances. Through the voice, the word and the sentence come to inhabit the liturgical space of the church, which is in itself a microcosm. Even the solitary projects his voice in space. This is not so much intended to resound *in* the world but rather to harmonize *with* the world. The cosmos was created by the Word, and it is through the incarnate Word that it was saved. Psalmody is singing with the Word, indeed in the Spirit of the risen Christ through whom the world, broken by sin, finds again harmony and cosmic beauty.

Very clearly in chant the singers are not centred on themselves and their voices. They try to act as genuinely as possible as part of a musical universe, shaped in harmony by the creating Word of God. In the words they pronounce and sing in unison, they recognize the Word of God who gives to his creation the just and harmonious proportions which find their expression and their measure in music.

The voice involves the body as the natural link between the individual and the cosmos. Harmony, which is the way the sounds resound with one another in the body and in space, proceeds from the adjustment between soul and body within the singer. This harmony will ultimately be conveyed through the psalmodic tones, that is, through the system of modality. In each mode, one principal note (or chord) is given the bulk of the text. Other notes can be used to underline the beginning of the phrase, to ornate the accent before the median pause and to signify the end of the phrase. The series of the notes which are being used is the scale. This can be very limited (for instance the minor third C–D–E around the chord of D in tone D), a little more extended (e.g. the fifth F–C in tone III) or reach nearly an octave (as in tone VII, G–F). The natural intervals of unison, third, fourth and fifth, always play a strong architectural role in the definition of each modal scale. The voice is guided by the melody within the scale of the mode, going from one degree to another either by enharmonic succession or by natural intervals. The melody is therefore both supple and solid. It develops freely within a structured space according to the rules of the so-called successive harmony.

The choice of privileged degrees in one scale leads to the recurrence of some intervals, while others are less used or totally excluded. The musical expression can be concentrated in certain modes on and around a single chord (horizontal structure). In others, however, the melody travels from the bottom to the top and back to the bottom of a bigger scale (bow-structure).

The different modes in their turn represent a panel of different moods. Each of them is harmonious, but they are harmonious in different ways and therefore resound in different manners in the soul and the body as well as in space. What might have appeared at first listening as a uniform landscape comes to offer with experience varied and differentiated scenery. In a manner which is not so different from the way the liturgical colours can contribute to the mood of a feast or a season of the liturgical year, the different modes express the varied moods of the Christian soul in prayer.

## Fear and joy

The voice of chant is the result of attentiveness to the words, their correct pronunciation and their natural rhythm in the sentence and in the verse, within the mood and harmony of the modal system. It does not want to 'show off' but simply to say, to pronounce in an appropriate way the sacred words of the Psalms. To this end, the voice needs above all to sing with the right spiritual attitude. Saint Benedict's teaching on psalmody in his Rule is very explicit on this point. For him, the whole climate of psalmody and chant is one of utter reverence towards God. He writes:

> We believe that the divine presence is everywhere and *that in every place the eyes of the Lord are watching the good and the wicked* (Prov. 15.3). But beyond the least doubt this is to be especially true when we celebrate the divine office. We must always remember, therefore, what the Prophet says: *Serve the Lord with fear* (Ps 2.11), and again, *Sing praise wisely* (Ps 46[47].8); and, *In the presence of the angels I will sing to you* (Ps 137[138].1). Let us consider, then, how we ought to behave in the presence of God and his angels, and let us stand to sing the psalms in such a way that our minds are in harmony with our voices.[4]

The 'fear of God', mentioned with reference to the second psalm, is the basic attitude for those who wish to sing 'wisely', and praise the Lord 'in the sight of the Angels'. It is the very root of this 'purity' already mentioned above. It guarantees that the singer does not put himself and his hopefully melodious voice in the forefront, but, on the contrary, seeks to insert himself into the harmony of God's work of creation, redemption and glorification. The most important task of the singer is to search for 'harmony' between 'mind' and 'voice'. In this way, he opens himself to the guiding and healing power of Christ, the Word of God. He is led from inside into God's glory. The way from fear of God to doxology is the Word himself who, by humbling himself and assuming humanity, reveals to the poor the mystery of the Father and so glorifies him.

This revelation is exultation and joy because it contains an infinite power of liberation. God's word is not fixed for ever in stone as an unchangeable, incomprehensible and unavoidable *karma*. It is endowed with the freedom of the Spirit. In the Spirit, the words sing. They are not a dead letter, but they are full of the life of the Resurrection. In the breath of God's Spirit giving life to the letter, the Word is movement.[5] It is the 'Word of life' (1 John 1.1), which is handed on by the Church to men and women of all generations in order to be given back to God in thanksgiving and praise. The tradition of the word, of which the tradition of the chant is part, is a work of the Spirit in the Church through generations of believers. In the chant, the word comes to those who sing and listen to it, clothed with the sober and lively line of music which expresses the movement of the word. This is not so much topographical as theological. It is the movement of the Word as expressed for instance in Isaiah:

> For as the rain cometh down, and the snow from heaven, and returneth not thither, but watereth the earth, and maketh it bring forth and bud, that it may give seed to the sower, and bread to the eater: So shall my word be that goeth forth out of my mouth: it shall not return unto me void, but it shall accomplish that which I please, and it shall prosper in the thing whereto I sent it. (Isa. 55.10-11, AV)

or the Prologue to the Fourth Gospel:

> In beginning was the Word . . . he came unto his own . . . the only begotten Son, which is in the bosom of the Father. (John 1.1, 11, 18, AV)

The simplicity of the chant gives a musical expression to this divine movement, leading the singers and hearers to an always deeper interiority and, at the same time, into the very heaven, to the Father who eternally pronounces the Word in love and with and in him, the whole universe.

### Vox Christi and ecclesiae

This theology of the Word and the voice cannot avoid making explicit the christological dimension of chant. The Psalms are 'vox Christi', according to Augustine's interpretation. Christ sings them not only as a single man in the incarnation, but as the head of the body, according to the teaching of the letters to the Ephesians and the Colossians. He is 'Christus Totus', the complete Christ, Christ with the Church, the two of them united in one voice as they are in one flesh.

Whereas we might have thought the Holy Spirit would inspire a new and properly Christian series of prayers for the needs of the Church, we can only observe that, at least in the Western part of the Church, Christian compositions were put aside soon enough. Then, constantly, as others reappeared, the Church reaffirmed her preference for the Psalms whose Christian meaning had been expounded by the fathers: Basil, Gregory of Nyssa, Chrysostom and Theodoret of Cyr in the East; Hilary, Ambrose, Augustine and Cassiodore in the West. Similarly, monasticism chose the Psalms and made of them the substance of the common prayer for coenobites, as it had been for solitaries before.

The true significance of chant cannot be understood without the reference to this teaching of the fathers. They expounded the meaning of the Psalms as the Christian prayer par excellence. What does it mean? Actually, the Psalms are the sung prayer of *Christus Totus*; that is, Christ and the Church. They are one in one voice, the voice of this body which is Christ's, which Christ animates totally and permeates with his life-giving Spirit. But we can also use another image: Christ and the Church are the Bridegroom and the spouse. Between them there is an exchange of love – the nuptial mystery that Paul describes in Ephesians 5 – which contains also an exchange of words which we could describe as a conversation. To quote again Pope Benedict's remarkably rich teaching on this matter:

> We ourselves are brought into conversation with God by the word of God. The God who speaks in the Bible teaches us how to speak with him ourselves. Particularly in the book of Psalms, he gives us the words with which we can address him, with which we can bring our life, with all its highpoints and low-points, into conversation with him, so that life itself thereby becomes a movement towards him.[6]

In the conversation between Christ and the Church, the conversation between God and man, disturbed and interrupted after the fall, is resumed and brought to perfection. Even the imperfections of the Psalms become part of it. To sing the Psalms is nothing other for the Church than to direct to Christ the words that his Spirit inspired in the Old Testament community so that he may assume them, as he did in his incarnation, and bring them to the perfection he is himself.

The movement of the chant – words and melody together – is in substance the 'movement towards' Christ that Pope Benedict describes. Chant is a loving answer of the Church to her divine Bridegroom. And here lies its essential beauty, which is not a question of aesthetics, but the irruption of the mystery in the world of senses. A simple antiphon and a basic psalmody can be more powerful than a rich polyphony perfectly sung because they do not stop at themselves but invite us to go always further, towards the well of eternal life in the heart of Christ from which the holy Church unceasingly draws the waters of life and the blood of redemption.

## Experience
### Tradition
The lifelong process of growth of Brother Harold's antiphonary can be taken as an apt metaphor for the process of a life with the chant. Chant was composed by dedicated singers who would learn it from childhood in the context of an oral tradition. The great majority of what we now sing as Gregorian chant had been composed before it began to be written down towards the end of the eighth century. Today we have books, and we sing from scores. Nevertheless, chant continues to work as it did when it was first composed. It works according to a process of assimilation. Even the less musical members of the monastic communities are able to make theirs the intervals and the modes of psalmody. This is the basis for all. As we have seen, more elaborate pieces develop within the pattern of psalmody. Indeed, a regular chanting of psalmody seems to be the best basis for an understanding 'from inside' and a natural assimilation of the rhythm of the words, the direction of the phrases and the modes of the pieces.

When you enter the monastery, you 'enter psalmody', as an old monk of Solesmes allegedly said. You begin a journey that is characterized by the repetition of the Psalms and the antiphons according to the cycles of the liturgical year. It is a very slow but steady process of growth. You seem to others – and sometimes to yourself as well – as if you are always doing the same thing, repeating the same psalms to the same God without any visible effect. At other times, the way leads you, beyond the desert, to oases of light, peace, joy, truth and beauty. The words seem to dance in your voice and to give the aptest expression of the exultant movement of your soul. Through these experiences of desolation and consolation, the chant becomes a faithful friend, able to accompany you on your journey with the Word of God. So, on some days, you would rather speak of the ascesis of the chant, putting up with the difficulties of an uneasy voice, the fastidiousness of the repetition or the struggle to sing in harmony with your brethren. But on other days, you love this companion to your prayer life more and more. He is utterly reliable, demanding but never in vain, simple and unpretentious and, as such, so adapted for the daily routine, while capable of sumptuous and intoxicating harmony and beauty.

A life with chant implies a growth into the nuptial intimacy with the Word, a penetration into the soul of the holy Church. In the end, it is about entering a tradition. This must not be understood only in the sense that we connect with what others before us have done for a very long time. It is not only about joining a venerable human tradition, even if this aspect is not without great value. It is above all about entering the movement of tradition as expressed in the teaching of Vatican II:

> This tradition which comes from the Apostles develops in the Church with the help of the Holy Spirit. For there is a growth in the understanding of the realities and the words which have been handed down. This happens through the contemplation and study made by believers, who treasure these things in their hearts (see Luke 2.19, 51) through a penetrating understanding of the spiritual realities which they experience, and through the preaching of those who have received through Episcopal succession the sure gift of truth. For as the centuries succeed one another, the Church constantly moves forward toward the fullness of divine truth until the words of God reach their complete fulfilment in her.[7]

Chant is fully traditional not so much because it has an old, long and venerable story, but because it enables each generation of singers to enter the – ultimately Marian – mystery of the growth of the Word in the Church. What is often described as the contemplative value of chant is nothing other than the participation it allows in the action of the Spirit expounding to the Church and to each soul the unfathomable riches of the mystery of the Word. Whoever understands that, will have no difficulty in concluding that in a contemplative life, chant enjoys pride of place. It does not mean that other musical styles are excluded. Brother Harold would dream of having a chamber organ in his chapel in order to give a polyphonic dimension to festive liturgies. Communities have successfully introduced sung polyphonies, either from the Western tradition or even borrowed from the Eastern liturgies. In the end, however, the criterion remains the place of the word and the orientation of the voice towards the word (and not the contrary).

## Beauty
Beauty comes as a result of formal perfection – which in the case of chant can be described as simplicity; that is, perfect and sober adaptation of the music to the text – but it does not stop at this level. Chant is intrinsically addressed to God, a tendency towards him who is both the origin of the words and the one who remains beyond them; chant is an answer to his presence in the midst of the Church. Chant is beautiful because it signifies his presence in a way that is very similar to architecture or to the icons. The key quality for singing chant is the right mood of holy fear and reverence, which come from the faith in and the feeling of God's presence. Benedict XVI explains it as follows:

> For Benedict, the words of the psalm: *coram angelis psallam Tibi, Domine* – in the presence of the angels, I will sing your praise (cf. 138:1) – is the decisive rule governing the prayer and chant of the monks. What this expresses is the awareness that in communal prayer one is singing in the presence of the entire heavenly court, and is thereby measured according to the very highest standards: that one is praying and singing in such a way as to harmonize with the music of the noble spirits who were

considered the originators of the harmony of the cosmos, the music of the spheres.[8]

In chant, the beauty of the eternal truth is given by Christ to his spouse the Church and given back by the Church to her Lord. 'Chant', says Brother Harold, 'points to the mystery.' That is why chant calls for a constant purification of the singer. A pure life, a pure voice and a pure praise go together. They lead the singer to the threshold of the mystery, the pure conversation of love between Christ and his Church:

Christ loved the church and gave himself up for her, in order to make her holy by cleansing her with the washing of water by the word, so as to present the church to himself in splendour, without a spot or wrinkle or anything of the kind – yes, so that she may be holy and without blemish. (Eph. 5.25-27)

## Doxology

Chant is music with the Word and music for the Word. Liturgy is a service of the Word with an orientation towards Eucharist; that is to say, towards the incarnate Word and all the consequences of incarnation: above all the Church, which is in the world, saved by the Passion and re-created in the Resurrection of Christ, giving glory to the Father.

Doxology is therefore the most profound reason for chant. In St Benedict's Rule, praise is emphasized as the motive for shaping the day with liturgy:

At these times, therefore, let us offer *praise* to our Creator 'for the judgements of His justice'; namely, at Lauds, Prime, Terce, Sext, None, Vespers, and Compline; and let us rise at night to *praise* Him (cf. Ps. 118[119]:164, 62).[9]

Praising the Creator and Saviour is the noblest thing a man or woman can do. We could here quote from Dom Guéranger's General Preface to *The Liturgical Year*:

Prayer is man's richest boon. It is his light, his nourishment, and his very life, for it brings him into communication with

God, who is light [St John viii. 12], nourishment [Ibid. vi. 35], and life [Ibid. xiv. 6]. But of ourselves we know not what we should pray for as we ought [Rom. viii. 26]; we must needs, therefore, address ourselves to Jesus Christ, and say to Him as the apostles did: 'Lord, teach us how to pray.' [St Luke xi. 1] He alone can make the dumb speak, and give eloquence to the mouths of children; and this prodigy He effects by sending His Spirit of grace and of prayers [Zech. xii. 10], who delights in helping our infirmity, asking for us with unspeakable groanings [Rom. viii. 26].

Now, it is in the holy Church that this divine Spirit dwells. He came down to her as an impetuous wind, and manifested Himself to her under the expressive symbol of tongues of fire. Ever since that day of Pentecost, He has dwelt in this His favoured bride. He is the principle of everything that is in her. He it is that prompts her prayers, her desires, her canticles of praise, her enthusiasm, and even her mourning. Hence her prayer is as uninterrupted as her existence. Day and night is her voice sounding sweetly in the ear of her divine Spouse, and her words are ever finding a welcome in His Heart.[10]

The Spirit, 'pneuma' (the very word from which is also derived the word 'neume' designating a note or a group of notes to be sung on one syllable and the written sign which express it), is at the source of the word as *prayer*. In the Spirit, the Church assumes the Word of God in all sorts of ways, from *lectio divina* to preaching. In the public life of the Church, chant represents the most intimate relationship of the body of the faithful with the word revealed to the full in the incarnate Word. It is, in the Spirit, an unsurpassed master of prayer and contemplation.

## Transfiguration

At the centre of the church at Shepherds Law, in front of the altar, a liturgical stand supports an icon of the transfiguration. Christ is manifested to the Church of the Old and New Testament in divine light as the objective presence of God's glory in this world and through the sign of his humanity. The vision though, magnificent as it may be, is not the highest revelation. From the cloud and the darkness, a voice invites to listen to the Word: 'Listen to Him'.

The icon has often traced its origin to the first part of this evangelical narrative with the painters trying to render the Taboric light and to suggest the presence of God's glory in this world. One could say that chant is an attempt to manifest the objective presence of Christ in his word. The chant says and sings the words not so much to deliver a message or to convey a doctrine or a theology as to indicate a presence. As the cherubim repeat the *Trisagion* and so designate the place of the presence of the one who cannot be circumscribed by any place, the Church sings the words that show the direction of the Word. He is hidden in the hearts of the singers, kept in glory in the bosom of the Father and manifested in the liturgy of the Church in word and Eucharist.

Chant does not meditate on the words, it does not comment on them, because it is enough to say the words, to point to the Word and to manifest the one who is present. The Church's only riches are Christ's presence among the believers as the people of God, as the holy Church, gathers in the Spirit to join in Christ's eternal prayer of intercession and to glorify the Father. It is one of the greatest joys on earth to take part in this manifestation and to be led by the chant of a psalm or of a simple antiphon to the place where the mystery of God's glory is revealed.

## Notes

1 Brother Harold Palmer, 'The Hermitage of St Mary and St Cuthbert, Shepherds Law, Northumberland', unpublished paper, July 2009.

2 'Est etiam in dicendo cantus obscurior', Cicero, *de Oratore* XVIII.

3 Pope Benedict XVI, Meeting with Representatives of the World of the Culture, Address, Collège des Bernardins, Paris, 12 September 2008. Available at http://w2.vatican.va/content/benedict-xvi/en/speeches/2008 /september/documents/hf_ben-xvi_spe_20080912_parigi-cultura.html.

4 *The Rule of St Benedict in Latin and English with Notes* [hereafter *RB*], Collegeville MN, Liturgical Press, 1981, Chapter 19, pp. 215–17.

5 As in the French word 'mot' (= word) derived from 'motus' (movement).

6 Benedict XVI, Address, Paris 2008.

7 *Dei Verbum* 8, in Austin Flannery OP (ed.), *Vatican Council II: The Conciliar and Post Conciliar Documents*, New York, Costello, 1988, p. 754.

8 Benedict XVI, Address, Paris 2008.

9 *RB* 16; our emphasis.

10 Abbot Prosper Guéranger, *The Liturgical Year*, trans. Dom Laurence Shepherd OSB, Fitzwilliam, NH, Loreto Publications, 2000, Vol. 1, pp. 1–2.

# 9

# Monastic Architecture and the Building of Shepherds Law: Monastic Life and Architecture

## CHRISTOPHER IRVINE
## AND RALPH PATTISSON

### Early monastic buildings

Irish monasteries could be assemblies of beehive huts; a Romanian one can look like a village; Monte Cassino is very different from Fountains: there is no blueprint for monastic architecture, no single or homogeneous style or design that has been adopted through the centuries and places and cultures. From the earliest days, it has been the pattern of life that has given rise to the best architectural arrangement and location in each particular place where monks and nuns have lived out their radical witness to the gospel. It has been the form of life that is lived,[1] periodically reformed, renewed and reinvigorated throughout Christian history, that has largely determined the setting, arrangement and design of monastic buildings.

The earliest written and archaeological evidence tells how the pioneers of the monastic movement[2] deliberately sought to distance themselves from the bustling urban centres where Christianity first established itself. Like Antony of Egypt in the fourth century, the desert mothers and fathers withdrew into the desert place. Significantly, though, they remained within reach of the increasing number of Christians who came to ask them for a word of wisdom: 'Father, give me a word.'[3] From the very beginning there was a tension between the need for solitude to nurture the things of the Spirit, and being in a place where the desert father or mother could be available for others as spiritual guide and companion. It is precisely this tension that has influenced the location where monks and nuns have chosen to live their life, and which eventually led to the development of the 'enclosure', the physical marking out of the monastery, or part of the complex of buildings, that provided the necessary silence for a recollected and singularly mindful life that was centred on God.

When Antony of Egypt (251–356) first heard the call of God he withdrew to the outskirts of the village in which he lived and then moved further away to Pispir in the Nile Delta, 50 miles south of the city of Memphis. For the later Irish monastics, such as Columba of Iona, the expanse of the sea became the equivalent of the desert place, and the Venerable Bede (672–735) tells us that the Northumbrian saint Aidan, a monk from Iona who founded a monastic community on the island of Lindisfarne, Holy Island, would periodically retreat further out to the Farne Islands. Recounting the siege and burning of Bamburgh, Bede tells us that at that time 'Bishop Aidan was living on Farne Island, which lies nearly two miles from the town, and which was his retreat when he wished to pray alone and undisturbed.'[4] This chosen location and setting of monastic life is significant and has deep echoes in the Christian tradition. The desert place, like the windswept islands off the Northumbrian coast, was a place that was both a place of testing (Exod. 17.7; cf. Ps. 95.8–9) and also a place of promise, as declared by the Hebrew prophets (e.g. Isa. 35.1–5).

When Antony became an old man, he withdrew even further into the wilderness, a good three-day journey to what is now known as St Antony's Mount. His biographer Athanasius (c.296–373) tells us that Antony '"loved the place", and that he settled there with its untended date palms, and made a garden'.[5] This was the place where Antony believed God was calling him to be, where he could live the life he was called to live and which spoke of the Christian's final hope of paradise. So the location and sense of place are integral to the ecology of monastic life, and this speaks directly to our contemporary situation of increasing social displacement and environmental crisis. The great father of Eastern monasticism, Basil of Caesarea (c.330–79), who placed the greatest value on life lived in community with others, wrote to his friend Gregory of Nazianzus around 361 to say that he had found the most beautiful location in which to live the monastic life and invited his friend to join him there.[6] Again, the place and location were not incidental to the form of life that they were seeking to live.

Together with the significance of location, there was also the marking out or delineation of the space. The monastic enclosure is a way of setting a boundary and defining the place, and interestingly this has parallels in prehistory, such as the making of the Avebury Ring in Wiltshire, and in other religious traditions, such as a Japanese Buddhist monastery. A fascinating example is the double-walled enclosure of the sixth/seventh-century monastery settlement that was built on Skellig Michael, a small, fairly inhospitable and storm-battered island some 20 kilometres off the coast of County Kerry in Ireland. This settlement had a double wall, creating both an inner and outer enclosure. It seems fairly unlikely that a remote site such as this required walls for defensive reasons, which rather suggests that the primary function of the walls was the zoning of the space. The inner wall encloses a series of buildings that include individual drystone beehive-shaped monks' cells, a larger community space of similar design and a small church or oratory. The material for building was in plentiful supply on the island, and the outer enclosure included a garden and a cemetery. More commonly in Ireland, and at Lindisfarne during the time of St Cuthbert (c.634–87), the monastic buildings were constructed with wood, and were surrounded by ditches and earth banks.[7] These banks and walls provided a measure of protection, delineated the space and created a definable and inhabited place.

It is very likely that the model that most informed the Irish monastic settlements of the fifth and sixth centuries was that of Pachomius of Egypt (292–346). A former soldier and convert to Christianity, Pachomius became a disciple of the desert fathers, and then, by deploying his considerable organizational skills he shaped a more corporate form of monastic life on a very large scale. Pachomius established his first monastic settlement in the abandoned village of Tabennisi in upper Egypt on the banks of the Nile.[8] The monastic settlement had an enclosing wall and an assortment of buildings. Each 'house' accommodated around 24 monks, and at the centre of the compound was an oratory, or church. This must have been of a considerable size as the whole commune would gather together twice a day for a corporate office consisting of psalmody. On a comparable scale of building there was also a refectory, providing a common table for the simple vegetarian fare, and an infirmary for the sick and infirm, as well as a number of ancillary buildings, all within the enclosed space of the monastic settlement. The inclusion of a gatehouse in the Pachomian monastery clearly regulated the flow of people in and out of the complex of buildings and suggests that its function was not so much to exclude but to mark out the place as being in some sense a special, or even a sacred, inhabited space. Some 45 years or so after Pachomius, Martin of Tours (316–97) established what was to become an influential monastic settlement at Liguge, in the fertile Loire valley. The impression given by his biographer, Sulpicius Severus, is that of an enclosed area containing individual cells for the monks, a series of small chapels and a single refectory for shared common meals.[9]

## Benedict and his Rule

The whole complex of monastic buildings within a defined space constitutes the monastery, the place where monastics live together in community.[10] The sense of a monastery being a sacred site is at least implicit in the sixth-century Rule of Benedict of Nursia, commended by Pope Gregory the Great, in Rome, as being a moderate monastic Rule. In the Rule the monastery is repeatedly referred to as the 'house of God', the *domus Dei*.[11] Here again is an enclosed site, but what is it, we might ask, that makes the monastery a sacred site? At the most obvious level it is the fact that the individual 'living stones' of the community place themselves before God so that they may become Christ's workmanship (Eph. 2.10).

The Rule is clear that the oratory, or church, is a holy place and that its primary purpose is the *opus Dei*, the corporate offering of the community's prayer and praise. It is the place where the community gathers to celebrate its corporate prayer, and at other times should be available for private prayer. It is for this reason that the space should not be used for any other purpose.[12] The same point is emphatically made in the Rule of St Augustine: 'The place of prayer should not be used for any purpose other than that for which it is intended and from which it takes its name.'[13] The oratory is a dedicated space, and the sense of it being a special place is implicit in what is said in the Rule about the disposition and behaviour of monks as they enter the oratory to perform the *opus Dei*. They are to be attentive, but above all to be conscious of the fact that what is said and sung in the oratory is said and sung in God's presence and before the angels.[14]

It is this sense of the oratory as a place of meeting and divine encounter that makes the place a holy place, but the question remains as to whether this sense of being a holy place extends to the whole monastery. The explicit point is that in the oratory, monks need to be conscious of the presence of God,[15] but the implication we could draw is that precisely because the community ought to be conscious of coming before God as they enter the oratory, so they should know that God is present in each space of the monastery and in the various activities that occur within them. As the Rule attests, 'We believe the divine presence is everywhere', and it then exhorts the monk to '. . . believe this most of all, without a trace of doubt, when we are present at the divine office'.[16] Perhaps an analogy begins to suggest itself here between the monastic life that involves the *whole* of a monastic's life and the sense of the presence of God pervading the whole monastery.

We can certainly take this as a hint that the monastery is a sacred site, and this again highlights the importance of the monastery's location and environmental impact. It would be anachronistic to read a heightened ecological consciousness back to the time of Benedict, but when he was compiling his simple Rule for Monks from other sources of Christian wisdom, Roman society was disintegrating and seriously unstable. There was a lack of political cohesion and an increasing threat of external invasion, and in this context the monastery was to be an oasis of communal living. In his own descriptive language, Benedict deployed the metaphors of 'workshop' and 'school', indicating that the monastery was primarily a place for the formation of Christian character. The Rule is known for its sense of proportion and for the humane allowances it makes for the limitations and proclivities of human nature, but it is equally attuned to the changing seasons of the natural year. It is this sensitivity to the cycle of the natural year that leads Benedict to adjust the daily pattern of the monk's day and his occupations according to the particular season of the year. Further, the following section of the Rule could be read as expressing sound ecological principles: 'If possible, the monastery should be set up so that all necessities – that is, water, a mill, a garden – are inside the monastic compound.'[17] There is certainly something about self-sufficiency in what is articulated here.

The Roman/Benedictine monastic model was taken to Northumbria by another Benedict, Benedict Biscop (c.628–690), who has been styled as the second founder of Western monasticism. He established his first monastery, dedicated to St Peter, at Monkwearmouth in 675. This became something of a model monastery and so King Egfrid gave further land for the building of a second monastery at Jarrow, and this was dedicated to St Paul, the second Apostle associated with Rome. Archaeological excavations of the site of the present parish church, directed by Rosemary Cramp in the 1960s and 1970s, have revealed a rectilinear ground-plan of the first monastic building on what was then a peninsula at Jarrow, with the Tyne and the Don flowing into the North Sea and forming two sides of the 'enclosure'. Originally the monastery consisted of two aligned, but separate churches built on an east–west axis, a series of monastic buildings running parallel to the two churches, a burial ground and a garden set out on a south-facing slope for the growing of basic necessities.[18] Jarrow is well known as the monastery in which Bede, the chronicler of the ecclesiastical history of the English people, was educated, and in his great work he records Benedict Biscop's trips to Rome. These were long and perilous journeys, and Bede records how on more than one occasion Biscop returned to Northumbria with people who were skilled in the practice of the liturgical arts and crafts. As noted above, the earliest Irish monastic buildings were constructed of wood,[19] but Benedict brought skilled stonemasons and glassmakers to Northumbria from Francia and Gaul to construct his twin Northumbrian monasteries. The churches were built of stone, probably taken from abandoned Roman sites in the vicinity, and according to the primary sources, the nave and roof at Wearmouth were decorated with paintings of New Testament scenes. The ancillary buildings, such as the dormitory and the refectory, were probably built of timber and had thatched roofs.[20]

The communities Benedict founded were centred on the liturgical celebration of the daily offices in the oratory or church. The church was built to serve the sound of sung prayer and praise, and it was Benedict Biscop who famously brought John the 'arch-chanter' from Rome to teach the chant to the monks of Northumbria and further afield.[21] The twin monasteries of Jarrow and Wearmouth were soon established as places of study and the making of books. In the early eighth century, Benedict's successor, Coelfrith, commissioned the writing of a single-volume Bible, the *Codex Amiatinus* in the monastic scriptorium. This was the largest book to be made in north-west Europe, and it was intended to be a gift for the Pope. The probably better known Lindisfarne Gospels, possibly made before AD 700, were splendidly illustrated by the monk Eadfrith at St Aidan's monastery on Holy Island, and these Gospels and the *Amiatinus* underline how the scriptoria and libraries were significant spaces which facilitated the love of learning. But monasteries were not inviolate. Both Wearmouth and Jarrow were attacked by Viking raids in the eighth century, and they were both eventually abandoned as a result of the Danish invasion in the ninth century.

## Monastic building patterns

There is a resilience to the monastic spirit, and it was apparently imprinted on the mind of Continental Christianity. This is vividly seen in the so-called Plan of St Gall. This elaborate plan was drawn up by a scribe at the monastery at Reichenau in Switzerland around 820. It was attached to a letter from Abbot Haito of Reichenau (763–836) to Abbot Gosbert of St Gall. The letter states that the annotated plan is sent for the recipient's consideration and as a demonstration of the author's devotion. The plan, or more precisely a copy of a plan, is not to be confused with what today we would regard as an architect's drawings. So what exactly is it? It could have been intended to be a diagram of the ideal monastery, but what is considered to be more likely is that it was a diagrammatical model of the monastic life. And as such it was an aid to reflection, allowing the recipient to internalize the significance of the place where silence is cultivated and where their balanced life of work, prayer and worship is lived out. In this sense, the plan is an aid for meditation, a model for conscious and prayerful reflection on the monastic life. Mary Carruthers has convincingly argued that the St Gall Plan was intended to be used as a *picture* or mental map that monastics could use to read the meaning of monastic life.[22]

At the centre of this comprehensive plan is a single and substantial church, and it seems likely that the whole arrangement was inspired by Gregory the Great's Homilies on the visionary prophet Ezekiel, for whom the temple at Jerusalem was the fount of God's salvation flowing out into the world. These homilies were a staple part of the monk's *lectio divina*, the slow reflective reading of sacred texts. The plan shows the arrangement of buildings and spaces within the monastic settlement. The drawing of the church is particularly detailed and shows the position of altars, doors and processional routes. The position and scale of the other buildings – the sacristy, scriptorium, dormitory, refectory, infirmary, novitiate and school – are also specified, and these are shown to be connected to each other via the cloister adjacent to the church on the south side. The cloister, from the Latin word *claustrum*, literally means an enclosed space, and it is in the centre of the plan. In terms of scale, the church is the most dominant of the buildings and is deliberately cross-shaped, with transepts at the north and south, recalling the intentional placing of monastic life in the paschal mystery of Christ's death and Resurrection.[23]

Monastic life is part of the DNA of Christianity, and it seems as though forms of monastic life emerge and re-emerge in different epochs of the history of Christianity. And perhaps the most famous and enduring example of this was the establishment of the Benedictine monastery at Cluny in Burgundy.[24]

Around 909 the dying Duke William III of Aquitaine gave a gift of an estate in the Rhone Valley for the establishing and building of a new monastery which, in line with the earlier Carolingian reform led by Benedict of Aniane (d.821) was to be strictly Benedictine. The abbey was to be free from both external ecclesiastical and royal interference and control, and was to be answerable to no other authority than the Pope himself. To make the point, the abbey was placed under the protection of the apostolic saints of Rome, Peter and Paul. The desire to return to a strict observance of the Rule of Benedict was taken by its founding abbot, Berno (850–927), from Baume Abbey, and his gifted protégé, Odo (d.942) who succeeded him as the Abbot of Cluny and who is credited with establishing Cluny as a centre of liturgical excellence, prayer and monastic formation.

The monastery and church at Cluny were rebuilt twice throughout a long history, and it is customary to refer to the three monastic churches as Cluny I, II and III. The second build was undertaken during the abbacy of the scholarly Mayeul, in 955. The monastic complex now included a chapter-house for the daily gathering of the community to hear the Rule being read and possibly for the giving of directions about the day's business. The rebuilt abbey church had a narthex at the west end,[25] providing additional space for stational or processional liturgy, during which the monks would pause to pray specifically for the departed in the Galilee Chapel, so named because of the direction given to the Apostles in Mark's Gospel that they were to return to Galilee and there encounter the risen Christ (Mark 16.7). The heart of the church – what we could describe in Benedictine terms as the workshop for the *opus Dei* – was the monastic choir, and it has been suggested that the aisles of the nave had stone tunnel vaulting to enhance the acoustic and serve the resonant singing of Gregorian chant in the choir.[26]

The monastery was substantially rebuilt during the long abbacy of Odilo (994–1049) to accommodate 75 monks. The new buildings achieved architectural distinction and included a refectory, dormitory, scriptorium (for the writing and illustration of books), novitiate and a guesthouse. The final church, Cluny III, of which only the south arm of a transept remains, was begun alongside the footprint of the old church in 1086, and by its completion under Abbot Hugh in 1120, was the largest ecclesiastical building in Europe between the twelfth and sixteenth centuries. There were two architects, both monks of Cluny, one of whom was a musician, reminding us again that the architecture of the church was the architecture of sound. From the outset, Cluny had embellished the liturgy with elaborate chant and ceremony, and as increasing numbers of monks were priests, they required their own altar to offer Mass, a practice that led to the proliferation of altars in monastic churches.

## Monasteries in England

The southern part of England witnessed something of a monastic revival in the late tenth century, led by Ethelwold, later Bishop of Winchester, Dunstan, Abbot of Gloucester and later Archbishop of Canterbury, and Oswald, Bishop of Worcester and founder of Ramsey Abbey in 969. Dunstan re-established monastic life in Glastonbury under the Benedictine Rule in 940, and it seems as though Ethelwold and Oswald may themselves have had architectural skills and may have been involved in rebuilding and the design of new monasteries.[27] Indeed, the history of the building of monasteries is a history of rebuilding and renewal. Within a period of 30 years following the refounding of monastic life at Glastonbury, for example, there were as many new or re-established monasteries in southern England. As David Knowles so eloquently and amply demonstrated in his classic study of English monasticism, it was these monasteries that became powerhouses of prayer, seedbeds of Christian culture and schools for the future leadership of the Church.[28]

This renewal of monastic life in England was endorsed by a meeting of abbots convened in Winchester around 970, which resulted in the promulgation of the *Regularis Concordia*,[29] a monastic agreement described by one writer as 'a symphony of rules which shows traces of the model of Cluny',[30] to regulate the life of monks and nuns in England. The motive in drawing together monastic Rules and customaries was not only to produce a coherent gameplan for the monastic life, now firmly under royal patronage, but also to give greater prominence to Benedict of Nursia and his Rule as its inspiration. One extant manuscript of the *Concordia* has two decorated miniature illustrations, and one of these shows King Edgar with Archbishop Dunstan and Bishop Ethelwold on either side, holding the scroll of the composite Rule.[31] The task of the monk was evidently to pray for the king and the good ordering of society, and to take his place in choir for the corporate celebration of the offices. As well as setting out the administration and ordering of monastic households, great detail was also added to the *Concordia* on how the Church's feasts and festivals were to be celebrated. It included an office for the dead and a celebration of the feast of All Saints, suggesting the influence of Cluny. In many respects the document serves as a monastic handbook, and it is a vital source for learning how the church building was consecrated and used liturgically, particularly in Holy Week and at Easter. Much can be inferred of the architectural plan from these liturgical directions, particularly regarding the significance of altars and relics, and the axial arrangement of the church, with the west end in some respects mirroring the east end in terms of its designated sacred space.[32] These spaces were enhanced by the liturgical arts, including metalwork which was personally promoted by Dunstan in the monastic workshops.

A further wave of reform was to break two centuries later. At this time, the level of decoration in carving, glass and polychrome statues and wall paintings became a matter of contention. This new wave of monastic reform was instigated in the twelfth century by the first Cistercians, whose initial intention was simply to return to the rigours of the Rule of Benedict. Their form of life was to be shaped by the three Benedictine elements of *opus Dei* – the round of daily prayer, *lectio* (meditative reading) and *labor manuum* (manual labour)[33] – but it is in the design and sparse decoration of the Cistercian church and cloister that we see the refinement of an interior monastic spirit and a developing monastic aesthetic.

## The Cistercian revolution

The story of the Cistercian reform begins with two key figures, the Englishman Stephen Harding and Alberic who shared Robert Abbot of Molesme's desire to withdraw further into the wooded marshland of Burgundy in order to live a more rigorous form of monastic life. This led to the establishment in 1098 of a new monastic household at Cîteaux, governed by a strict application of the Rule of Benedict. From there the 'white monks', as they were called, established another house, made famous by Bernard at Clairvaux. Bernard wrote in a reasoned critique that decoration and vividly painted statues of saints can easily draw the eye and distract the monks from their prayer. And then in a more rhetorically charged passage, Bernard delivers a hard-hitting critique of Romanesque abbeys: 'The walls of the church are ablaze with light and colour while the poor of the Church go hungry . . . money for feeding the destitute goes to feast the eyes of the rich',[34] only to be tempered later with an allusion to the beauty of holiness. Given the rhetorical nature of the sources, perhaps the differences between the how the 'black monks' and 'white monks' lived was exaggerated.

Nevertheless, there were differences in what today would be termed theological aesthetics. What we see in Cistercian architecture is certainly a reduction of colour in painting and glass, but in terms of architectural elevations and fenestration, the

Cistercian aesthetic was expensive and deeply nuanced. And as one scholar has suggested, although there were some regional differences, there was similarity in the ground-plan and architecture of Cistercian monasteries.[35] The monumental Cistercian abbeys in the north of England at Fountains and Rievaulx built in the valleys of the Yorkshire moors, with their soaring arches and capacious cloisters, may not have mirrored the luxurious and jewel box colours of the heavenly Jerusalem. Nevertheless, they were architecturally striking and came to represent the holy city,[36] established even on the remote frontiers of the then inhabited world. The rapid expansion and growth of Cistercian abbeys, even within the span of Bernard's lifetime (1091–1153) in England and on the Continent was astonishing, and is a testimony to how the Rule of Benedict, that wellspring of Christian wisdom, is able to renew and reform monastic life at different times and in different circumstances.

The Cistercian church and its adjacent cloister echoed the architectural arrangement of the ancient Roman villa with its enclosed central atrium, and it connected the ancillary communal buildings on a single grid and provided the heart of the Cistercian monastery. Here with each hour there was an almost continuous flow from an individual reflective silence to corporate worship and back again through the night and day of the monk's life. Here the holy city was a silent city, attuned to God and constantly in an undistracted conversation that was voiced in corporate prayer and praise in the offering of the *opus Dei* and the Mass. The architectural design of the abbey and its church, with the play of light and shade in its buildings, conspired to create an ideal environment for both the cultivation of an interior life and a corporate voicing of praise to the Creator.[37]

The church at the centre of the monastery was again cruciform in its ground-plan. Its architecture was elegantly simple and provided clear sightlines, although it is interesting to note that the east end of the Abbey at Clairvaux was extended with a chevet (a semicircular east end of the church) even when Bernard was still alive.[38] The innovation in this renewed form of monastic community life was the inclusion of lay brothers who were employed in the heavier work of cultivating what was previously an uncultivated and wild landscape. The lay brothers were illiterate and gathered for regular simple devotions in the nave of the abbey church, whereas the monks occupied the monastic choir for their offices. The interior of the church was thus simply divided, east and west, choir and nave. In these abbey churches a narthex was often constructed at the west end, and in daytime the east end was often flooded with direct sunlight. Doors, both south and southwest, connected the church to the cloister. And as in the interior of the church, with the exception of the painted wooden statue of the Blessed Virgin Mary, the cloister lacked statuary, and figurative carved capitals were prohibited. The four-square cloister was generally built on the south side of the building to catch the light and was used primarily for para-liturgical activities, such as the assembling for communal processions in and out of the church and for the washing of feet on Saturday evenings, as well as other contemplative purposes. At the centre of the cloister garth, or green space, there was often a well or a fountain. Grisaille glass (a tinted glass) was deliberately used in both the abbey church and the chapter-house, and this was seen as a way of filtering that pure natural light that was considered to be essential for inner enlightenment. Unsurprisingly, light came to be deployed as a key metaphor for the transcendence of God and the truth of Christ in the work of Cistercian writers such as William of St Thierry and Aelred of Rievaulx.

At this point in our discussion of the monastic form of life and its architecture, a further note may be added about monastic vocation. This vocation mimics that of the psalmist who, being invited to 'seek [God's] face', answered, 'your face, LORD, do I seek ' (Ps. 27.8). Such a seeking after God may well be served by what we could describe as a generous architecture, an architecture that enables the monk to reimagine how we dwell and inhabit space. The monastery should give people space both to be alone and to be with others in an increasingly cramped, overcrowded and atomized social world. It provides both the space where the monk can place himself before God and also the space where he may encounter Christ in the welcome of guests. The monastery needs, quite simply, to be spacious, giving space to in-breathe the Spirit and to enable those who live and visit the place to pray again with the psalmist '[God has] brought me out into a broad place' (Ps. 18.19a).

## Elements of a monastic building

From this brief overview of monastic life and sketch of its buildings, we are able to extrapolate and enunciate a number of discrete points in relating what is required for the living of monastic life and of monastic architecture in terms of the monastery buildings and their overall design. These points are listed here, but not in any order of importance:

- The buildings need to facilitate the common life of the community.
- The church should be at the centre, should be conspicuous architecturally and should 'celebrate God'.
- The church needs to be sufficiently spacious, beyond that which is required to accommodate the community and its guests.
- The monastery should safeguard the place of silence in the enclosure.
- Gates, doors, pathways and processional routes need to be considered as part of the general plan of the complex.
- Facilities for welcoming and accommodating guests need to be provided.
- The monastery as a site of pilgrimage needs to be considered.
- The artwork in the monastery requires strong design and should be made of good-quality materials.
- Attention should be given as to how the monastery sits in the natural landscape in which it is set.
- Consideration should be given to both the ecology of the monastic form of life and the ecological footprint of the buildings.
- Consideration should be given to what needs to be provided for the monastery to be a place for educational and intentional Christian formation.
- Facilities should speak of the community's commitment to serve the poor and to promote social justice.

This is certainly not an exclusive list of the multifarious activities that might properly take place within the monastic complex, but the architect of a monastic building needs to be adequately briefed and have a good sense of what it is that occurs in a monastery. As John Pawson, the architect of the stunning new Cistercian monastery of Novy Dvur in the Czech Republic insists, true significance is to be attributed to what we actually do in a particular architectural space. Here he is thinking of the daily rituals that take place in the different spaces within the monastery and how they should inform the overall design of the building. The activity, in other words, is primary. So what happens in the church, singing for instance, is, as all worship should be, directed beyond itself to the triune God and so needs to resound. And further, as the church is more than a shelter to accommodate the community and its guests, its physical volume and proportions should articulate the sense of the divine transcendence in our midst, which is invoked and responded to in our acts of worship. Of course, it is equally true that God, being everywhere, can be worshipped by Christians gathering together anywhere, but the physical building in which a community gathers can express something of the holiness of God and speak of the goal of Christian pilgrimage. For the triune God is a God who enters and encounters us in time and space, and thereby, as Thomas Torrance has argued, binds us even in our relationship with God to space and time.[39] The church building should both ground us as the place of encounter and response to the divine presence, and also announce in its very form and design, its scale and through its particular architectural features such as towers and spires, that the transcendent cuts into and enters even the built environment of our world. The breaking-in of the transcendent in our midst should also be evident in the ordering and furnishing of the interior liturgical space. The altar, for instance, should be prominent and make the visual statement that Christ, who calls, gathers and feeds us at his table, is present in our midst. And if Christ is present, the design of the altar should be bold, and if Christ is, as one New Testament metaphor suggests, our 'rock', stable and utterly reliable, then there should be a solidity in its design.[40] Other aspects of the dynamic of worship can also be expressed in the ordering and design of liturgical foci. The lectern or ambo, for instance, could be placed in the centre of the gathered community to illustrate the essential dialogical dynamic of worship, of how it is the Word who calls and speaks, and is the one to whom we respond in the utterance of prayer and in voices raised in song.

How monasteries are built is an index of what we believe about God, of who we think God is, and the design of the building and the materials used in its construction should celebrate God and transcend the purely utilitarian. We have already hinted at how the architectural massing and volume may give significance to a building, but perhaps there are three other essential features of an architecture of transcendence.

Simplicity of line and form best serve the monastic goal of cultivating the inner life, but this is achieved by a deliberate design process of simplification, rather than just a minimalist style. The volume of a building gives it a sense of spaciousness, and this is beneficial not only in the monastic church, where there is a sense of being met by the God whose reality is, as the scholar monk Anselm insisted, greater than we might think or imagine, but also in relation to the whole complex. If the refectory is to be a place of hospitality, it too has to be a room of spacious proportions. Similarly, the living-quarters of the community itself should be sufficiently spacious to give each monk ample space to be and to move easily through the linking corridors of the building.

The significance of space has emerged as a recurring theme in this discussion, and together with space, there is also the element of light. It has been said of the Abbey of Our Lady at Novy Dvur that the architect has effectively created what has been described as architecture of light.[41] This feature, though often overstated, is a vital element in monastic architecture. Light reveals the form of a building, and windows in the church and cloister have a function beyond the utilitarian in allowing for the interplay of inside and outside, enclosure and setting. The symbolic charge of light coming into the enclosed space of a church has a particular religious resonance. As Richard Kieckhefer argues, the play of light on its floors and walls has a significance that is beyond the architectural.[42] Indeed, the shifting patterns and intensity of direct and diffused light may well conspire to signal the breaking-in of transcendence, and may be an invitation to the worshipper to approach the one 'who dwells in unapproachable light' in the mystery of worship. An example of this is seen in the interior of the Abbey Church of St Sixtus of Westvleteren, in Belgium, which was designed by the renowned Flemish architect bOb van Reeth (sic). The project began in 2005 and was completed in 2012.

A band of patterned glazing, above the suspended wooded frame of the ceiling, allows the constantly shifting direct sun and diffused skylight to play on the brick walls and floor of the building through the hours of the day from dawn to dusk. The constantly shifting pattern of light in the chapel makes it a most appropriate space for the marking of time, the celebration of the regular monastic hours of prayer. Each moment of time is taken up into eternity as the *opus Dei* punctuates the movement from night to day and through the day back into the silence of the night.[43]

## Monastic location

As we have seen, the location of a monastery is not incidental. Location matters, and we have alluded to monasteries located on windswept moorland, on the edge of dense woodland and on a promontory pointing out to sea. All these examples speak of the intention to bring order and harmony to what appeared to be inhospitable and difficult terrain. The twelfth-century Benedictine monk and chronicler William of Malmesbury (d.1142) commenting on Thorney Abbey, an Anglo-Saxon monastery built on the watery fens between Spalding and Ely, speaks of the monastery in terms that are reminiscent of the biblical promise of the blossoming of the wilderness:

> In the middle of wild swampland where the trees are intertwined in an inextricable thicket, there is a plain with very green vegetation which attracts the eye . . . here the earth bears fruit trees, there grapevines cover the ground or are held on high trellises.[44]

Despite the rhetorical exaggeration of William's description, this is far from being a romantic feeling of oneness with nature. The monks were very aware of the harsh conditions in which they lived, and of the sheer physical struggle of cultivating fields and gardens in difficult terrain. Nevertheless, the choosing of a location was very deliberate, and the more difficult the terrain, the more appropriate it seemed as the site in which to restore something of paradise.

In our own times, this has been exemplified to some extent in the building of the new Abbey for the Benedictine nuns of Stanbrook Abbey, Worcestershire. The new abbey church was dedicated on 6 April 2015.[45] The new site was eventually chosen on the North York Moors, fairly close to the sites of the former Cistercian abbeys at Byland and Rievaulx. The community were determined that their new abbey should be ecologically friendly and that its design should be compatible with the landscape. This was effectively delivered by the architect Feilden Clegg, and it is built with locally sourced stone and sustainable seasoned oak timber. Energy is captured by solar panels, and the convent roof is covered with sedum grass so that it blends with the natural environment. In 2016, the abbey was shortlisted for a regional RIBA award. The pinnacle of the sacrament chapel rises steeply from the chapel roofline and at its highest elevation it has a large cross-shaped window, which, like the open glazed cloister, connects the inside of a contemplative space to the outside environment.

Having sketched out some of the general features of monastic life and architecture in rather generalist terms, it is now time to turn to the building of Shepherds Law in Northumberland and the story of its conception, design and building, which is written by its architect, Ralph Pattisson.

## The concept

> I was by his side, a master craftsman,
> delighting him day after day,
>     ever at play in his presence,
> at play everywhere in his world,
>     delighting to be with the sons of men. (Prov. 8.30–31, JB)

> Man's heart makes the plans,
> Yahweh gives the answer. (Prov. 16.1, JB)

To design a chapel at the turn of the twentieth century when you have been conditioned at school in the 1950s and attended architecture school in the 1960s – that is and was a challenge. The client, Brother Harold Palmer, gave me a brief about how he envisaged the use of the building and how he saw that usage in practice. The trustees, holding the purse strings, knew how small it had to be (the original scheme was substantially reduced in size). The crux was: how could the sacred nature of a space be described in building (architectural) terms? That was the all-embracing question. Earlier, I had admired the clean lines and no frills of the Modern Movement and had studied books on liturgy and architecture and designed a few alterations and additions to halls and churches to improve their form and function as places of worship. The problem was always the same – the fussiness of gothic arches and boring brick and stone and stained glass – all the 'churchiness' which was being discounted by young minds seeking deep-down awesomeness without the baggage of past generations of believers, and yet keep with the best from what had been before. How to do that, even in a small way and on a remote hillside, that was the question.

Furthermore – what a location (Figure 1)! At OS map reference, NU087166, named 'SHEPHERDS LAW', there were some substantial eighteenth-century ruins: a strong wall running east–west and some fine round-headed blind arches facing west with square towers at the ends, one partially demolished, and other works and remains forming a rectangle some 70 × 45 metres. The site lies in upland pasture and gorse and scrub with mature scots pine and a stand of ash by a duck pond. The place lay halfway up a hillside rising to the south and west with panoramic views to the north

*Figure 1. The construction of the chapel showing its setting in the landscape.*

*Figure 2. Eighteenth-century arcading on perimeter wall.*

and north-west of low-lying rolling Northumberland arable and pasture with the border rising in the distance along the ridge of the Cheviot Hills. It was the kind of location that makes a big impression and reaction in the mind of an architect (or anyone else for that matter) and raises a huge challenge to achieve something which tries to do justice to the site and is fit for purpose.

In 1985 Brother Harold had built, under my direction, part of an overall development plan (Figure 3), which included a chapel, a cloister and some cells or living accommodation for single people visiting. Alongside this were workshops and a library in one of the towers. Four cells were built along the north wall, with the south-facing length of cloister or passage alongside leading to Brother Harold's hermitage, which he had built previously. His original hermitage displayed a palette of materials and principles for the whole new project. He used recycled stone, concrete and block to make thick walls with narrow tall windows and steep pitched roof (50°) covered in rich red clay pantiles salvaged from farm buildings long neglected and available locally. When Brother Harold's mother died in 1997, she left funds with the Society of St Francis at Alnmouth (where Brother Harold had been part of the community until he received a calling to become a hermit) with the express wish that a chapel be built at Shepherds Law. Thanks to the advice of Christopher Downs, architect to Durham Cathedral, I was given a renewed commission to design the chapel as proposed on the original development plan for Shepherds Law from 1985.

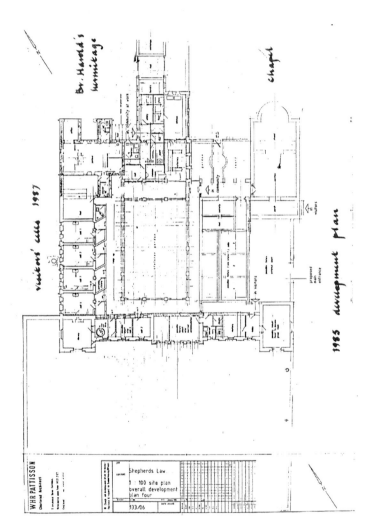

*Figure 3. Ralph Pattisson's architectural drawings for the whole site at Shepherds Law.*

*Figure 4. Beltry and church from the west.*

Brother Harold did a sketch showing an amorphous shape with prominence of altar, lectern and celebrant's chair round a kind of enclosure. He also produced some notes of his from 1964 and many books and photographs of Romanesque churches and chapels, pointing out the features which appealed to him most. These included details of stonework and openings and roofs where great coherence and simplicity had been achieved. We visited a number of local churches including Old Bewick nearby with its fine proportions and beautiful vaulted apse. Durham Cathedral with its stone on stone – no wooden beams but vaulted stone roof which gives such unity to the whole. These were some fundamental pointers and directions of endeavour for the chapel.

In practical terms, Brother Harold had accumulated a large quantity of stone given by neighbouring farmers and landowners.

*Figure 5. Church and cells from the south west.*

We made a trip with some architects and student architects to the south bank of the river Breamish and selected and loaded stone on to a cart from there. When the chosen builder, Mr Donaldson of Seahouses, built a sample wall, I asked and suggested that the size of the stones selected should be the largest available, and he responded with great alacrity and skill. When he selected stones, he would choose an existing face, shaping the sides as little as possible leaving no sharp or straight saw-cuts exposed and finishing all arises by hand. The result is that the walling with original tooling and moss and lichen looks as though it has been in place for ever. We had noticed that some of the most attractive façades had built into the stonework random pieces of terracotta tile or brick, lightening the masonry and adding interest and colour. In this vein, we gathered sea-washed bricks and tiles that had come from a rubbish dump on Lindisfarne and were washed away by high seas and ended up on the seashore by St Cuthbert's Island. We picked up some pieces in plastic bags and delivered them to Jim Donaldson to be used as galleting where appropriate. He approved of the idea and found the pieces useful for gap filling.

## The design

With regard to the actual design, the overriding consideration was the coherence of material. Why was Durham Cathedral, especially the Norman nave, so very impressive? Because of stone on stone everywhere. The floor was stone, the walls and pillars were stone, the arcading was stone, the ribs and vaulting were stone. Everything was coherent and detailed in stone. The benches and seating and lighting (of course) were later additions, accretions really. Also Durham had string courses (Figure 6), horizontal projecting courses of stone which lead the eye round the building. And the walls were thick, very thick. This allowed the play of light to fall on several recesses or orders of depth outside and in with deep and wide angled reveals allowing sunlight to have its effect as it passed from outside to the interior.

At Shepherds Law, some concern was expressed about the proposed six narrow window openings lighting the body of the chapel (too small to be called a 'nave'). They were 178mm, seven inches wide, three on the south side and three on the north. The concept was vindicated in the result – the contrast of natural light into an

*Figure 6. The interior string course.*

unusually gloomy interior giving a strong sense of difference or perhaps transcendence, separating it from the spaces of everyday living. However, Brother Harold did suggest light from the west to catch the evening sun, and four small openings were added during building work, slotted in above the narthex roof and below the engineer's concrete ring beam, and they add a richness to the interior on sunny afternoons and evenings.

To add some grandeur to this little building, we designed four brick arches of the same radius over a central crossing with a heavy square stone tower above with slit windows at high level and a four-square hipped roof of low pitch pantiles set in mortar against the wind with a special wrought iron cross at the peak. We produced a strong shadow line at the eaves but no gutter, allowing rain water to be blown away. This detail adds solidity to the structure. Underneath the roof the soffit is boarded with exposed rafters and timber ties.

The body of the chapel and apse are vaulted in concrete block and rendered with a coarse grit self-coloured off-white sand/cement render floated on by skilled plasterers. The interior walls are similarly rendered block giving a sense of unity and coherence to the whole. Set in the side walls are six seats built into the thickness and corresponding to the slit window openings above. The apse was added under a separate contract four years later and much care and consideration was taken with the arrangement of the small openings and the brick and stone exterior details round the eaves. The pitched roof is half a cone and slated with Scottish 'peggies' or some slates, a preference of Brother Harold's brother over clay tiles. The side buttresses are substantial and a requirement of the structural engineer, Charles Blackett Ord. Any side chapel or vestry extension has yet to be built, hence the blocked external side arches. The stained glass in the apse was a special gift and is by Lorraine Lamond, who trained at the Glasgow School of Art. The remaining 13 lights are dalle-de-verre (slab glass) designed and made and installed by myself, the architect. The window in the apex of the narthex is by Douglas Hogg, a local stained glass artist, who trained at the Edinburgh School of Art, and was commissioned by Brother Harold.

The way the builder and mason, Jim Donaldson, chose and laid the exterior masonry tiles with stone and brick details is way beyond what my drawings and the contract required. That is to say, Mr Donaldson's skill as a master mason is fully displayed in this chapel both inside and out. The walls are 750 mm thick in the body and 900 mm in the apse, lending gravitas to a tiny building and good insulation from cold and heat. A special requirement of Brother Harold was a sloping floor down towards the altar steps (Figure 7). This was achieved with much scratching of heads and many revised drawings. The floor incorporates waterborne underfloor heating and sunken radiators flush with the floor. In the body of the chapel down to the steps, the floor is laid with terracotta tiles demarking where seating could be placed (normally there are no pews or chairs in this space), with stone paving round the sides and down the centre. The Indian stone has beautiful plant-like leaves embedded in it, which the floor-layer selected very carefully when he laid down the slabs. The water for the underfloor heating is fed through plastic pipework off a propane gas boiler sunk beside the porch on the north side. Electricity to control the boiler comes from a small wind generator and solar panels with a bank of batteries in the shed. Because the whole structure has such a great mass for a tiny space, very little energy is required to achieve a comfortable temperature or steady state. The thick block vault with pitched roof above with much insulation assists in this aim of conserving heat and protection from cold. Clay pantiles with eaves of a few courses of clay rosemary tiles were chosen to fit in

*Figure 7. The interior of the chapel.*

with the rural landscape. The clay from Grimsby near Hull was chosen for its rich orange/red hue. The gutters to the main roof are of aluminium, ogee section, allowed to oxidize (not painted) so as to minimize maintenance.

## The chapel

The chapel is low lying in the land with 230mm, nine-inch land drains running under and round the foundations and led away to the nearby duck pond. In addition, the landlord, Sir Ralph Carr-Ellison, allowed Brother Harold a ditch along the line of the higher ground to avoid the risk of flooding from occasional torrential rain storms. Initially side access was up the hill across fields or down the hill from the nearby reservoir track. However, a track was eventually cut into the hillside, thanks to the trustees, which helped for vehicular access in bad weather. The witness of Brother Harold to the gospel and the foundation of the Hermitage of St Mary and St Cuthbert attracts many visitors. Brother Harold rings a huge medieval bell at midday to signal prayers. He observes the monastic round of daily prayer and hopes soon to build the

*Figure 8. Cells forming cloister north walk.*

east side of the cloister connecting the chapel with the hermitage. This will be a great comfort and advantage when rain falls and winter winds and snow blow across the hill and through the site.

## Notes

1 See G. Bachelard, *The Poetics of Space*, trans. M. Jolas, Boston, MA, Beacon Press, 1969. The monastic form of life manifested itself in various forms, not only in its buildings, but also in composition. There were double monasteries of women and men, as at Whitby, and communities of both monks and secular clerks as, at various times, at Christ Church Priory in Canterbury. See Jesse D. Billett, *The Divine Office in Anglo-Saxon England*, Henry Bradshaw Society, London, Boydell Press, 2014.

2 I am using the word monastic as generic term from the word 'monos', which literally means 'alone', to include those who live the solitary life, technically known as the *eremitical* life, and those living in community, the *coenobitical* life.

3 Graham Gould, *The Desert Fathers on Monastic Community*, Oxford, Clarendon Press, 1993.

4 Bede, *Ecclesiastical History of the English People*, Chapter 16, London, Penguin Books, 1990, p. 168.

5 Athanasius *Life of Antony*, ch. 49 and 50, in Robert Gregg (ed.), *Athanasius: The Life of Antony and the Letter to Marcellinus*, Classics of Western Spirituality, Mahwah, NJ, Paulist Press, 1979, pp. 68-9.

6 Basil of Caesarea, *Epistle* 14, in Philip Schaff (ed.), *Nicene and Post-Nicene Fathers Series II*, Vol. 8, Edinburgh, T&T Clark, 1894, p. 124.

7 Mick Aston, *Monasteries in the Landscape*, Stroud, Tempus, 2000, p. 45.

8 Derwas J. Chitty, *The Desert as City*, Yonkers, NY, St Vladimir's Press, 1966, pp. 22–3.

9 Sulpicius Severus, *The Life of St Martin of Tours*, Putty, NSW, St Shenouda Monastery, 2013.

10 John Cassian, *Conferences*, No. 10, in Colm Luibheid (ed.), *John Cassian: Conferences*, Classics of Western Spirituality, Mahwah, NJ, Paulist Press, 1985, p. 191.

11 *The Rule of St Benedict* [hereafter *RB*], 31.19, 64.5. The edition used in this chapter was the one edited and translated by Bruce L. Venarde, Cambridge, MA, Harvard University Press, 2011.

12 *RB* 52.

13 *The Rule of St Augustine*, Chapter 2, trans. Raymond Canning OSA, London, Darton, Longman & Todd, 1984, p. 13.

14 *RB* 19.

15 *RB* 19.

16 *RB* 19.

17 *RB* 66.6.

18 D. M. Wilson (ed.), *The Archaeology of Anglo-Saxon England*, Cambridge, Cambridge University Press, 1976.

19 Kristina Kruger, *Monasteries and Monastic Orders*, ed. Rolf Toman, Potsdam: H. F. Ullmann, 2008.

20 Peter Hunter Blair, *The World of Bede*, Cambridge, Cambridge University Press, 1990, pp. 165–6, 172.

21 Bede, *Ecclesiastical History*, Chapter 18, p. 234.

22 Mary Carruthers, *The Craft of Thought: Meditation, Rhetoric, and the Making of Images, 400–1200*, Cambridge, Cambridge University Press, 1998, pp. 228–31.

23 Christopher Irvine, *The Cross and Creation in Christian Liturgy and Art*, London, SPCK, 2013, p. 126.

24 Marcel Pacaut, *L'Ordre de Cluny: 909–1789*, Paris, Fayard Press, 1986.

25 Nigel Hiscock, *The Wise Master Builder: Platonic Geometry in Plans of Medieval Abbeys and Cathedrals*, Aldershot, Ashgate, 2000, p. 159.

26 Allan Doig, *Liturgy and Architecture from the Early Church to the Middle Ages*, Aldershot, Ashgate, 2008, p. 158.

27 Hiscock, *Wise Master Builder*, pp. 161–3.

28 Dom David Knowles, *The Monastic Order in England: A History of its Development from the Times of St Dunstan to the Fourth Lateran Council 943–1216*, Cambridge, Cambridge University Press, 1949, pp. 49ff.

29 Richard W. Pfaff, *The Liturgy in Medieval England*, Cambridge, Cambridge University Press, 2009, p. 78.

30 Peter Levi, *The Frontiers of Paradise: A Study of Monks and Monasteries*, London, Collins Harvill, 1987.

31 See Lawrence Nees, *Early Medieval Art*, Oxford, Oxford University Press, 2002, p. 225.

32 See Helen Gittos, *Liturgy, Architecture, and Sacred Places in Anglo-Saxon England*, Oxford, Oxford University Press, 2013, and Doig, *Liturgy and Architecture*.

33 See the Cistercian recension of Benedict's Rule, the *Carta Caritatis*, Ch. 48.

34 'An Apologia for Abbot William', in Paula Matarasso (ed.), *The Cistercian World: Monastic Writings of the Twelfth Century*, London, Penguin Books, 1993, pp. 56–7.

35 Giles Constable, 'From Cluny to Citeaux', in Constable, *Cluny from the Tenth to the Twelve Centuries*, Aldershot, Ashgate, 2000, p. 320.

36 In *Epistle 64* Bernard claimed that Clairvaux mirrored the holy city, the heavenly Jerusalem. See *The Letters of St. Bernard of Clairvaux*, Stroud, Sutton Publishing, 1998.

37 Terryl Kinder, *Cistercian Europe: Architecture of Contemplation*, Kalamazoo, MI, Cistercian Publications, 2002, especially pp. 374, 383–5.

38 Emilia Jamroziak, *The Cistercian Order in Medieval Europe 1090–1500*, London, Routledge, 2013, p. 158.

39 T. F. Torrance, *Space, Time and Incarnation*, Oxford, Oxford University Press, 1969, p. 107.

40 See Crispino Valenziano, 'Liturgical Architecture', in Anscar J. Chupungco (ed.), *Handbook for Liturgical Studies*, Collegeville, MN, The Liturgical Press, 2000, p. 383.

41 *John Pawson: Themes and Projects*, London, Phaidon Press, 2004, p. 105.

42 Richard Kieckhefer, *Theology in Stone: Church Architecture from Byzantium to Berkeley*, Oxford, Oxford University Press, 2004, pp. 109–10.

43 For a historical exposition of the theology of the liturgy of the hours, see Gregory W. Woolfenden, *Daily Liturgical Prayer: Origins and Theology*, Aldershot, Ashgate, 2004.

44 Cited by Jean Leclercq, *The Love of Learning and the Desire for God: A Study of Monastic Culture*, London, SPCK, 1978, p. 165.

45 http://www.stanbrookabbey.org.uk/site.php?id=4.

# Waiting While Running

## GEORGE GUIVER

### Whose normality?

At the main meals in an Italian religious community, wine will usually be served: it is an everyday beverage to Italians, as tea is to the British. If a British community were to serve wine at every meal, however, this would raise eyebrows. Peter Berger has coined the phrase 'plausibility structures' to speak of cultural contexts in which some things become possible and others not.[1] The culture in Italy means it is entirely plausible to say wine will be an expectation at most meals. No one would be self-conscious or apologetic about it, whereas in Britain a religious community would. Berger uses this concept mainly in relation to religion, lamenting the fact that secularized, pluralistic society has undermined people's capacity to see religious faith as plausible, as something normal.

It might be helpful in our present discussion to adapt this and speak of 'normality-structures'. On the seafront at Margate it is unremarkable for a person to go around scantily dressed and even barefoot; in the centre of Huddersfield it would not look normal, and any reasonably sensitive person so attired should feel a little self-conscious. These are examples of what you might call cultural normality-structures.

The life of religious communities includes many normality-structures not to be found in everyday life, and one of them concerns worship. In my own Community of the Resurrection the daily services are non-negotiable. In a chapter discussion during my time as a novice, urgent attention was given to a crisis at our priory in Zimbabwe in the aftermath of the civil war: soldiers were on the roads, the Zimbabwean prime minister's office was in contact with the superior, a decision by the community was urgently needed. In the midst of a difficult discussion the bell rang and we needed to go to church for the midday office. Not only did we abandon the discussion in full flow, we moved smartly to church to get there on time. There were no guests or visitors – we were on our own – but that is what we did, because of an innate knowledge that this is what we do: you don't fit the liturgy around the life; the life has to fit around the liturgy. To an outsider this could look barmy; the only way to understand this behaviour is to come inside the normality-structure by giving yourself to this way of life. One monastic principle, clearly set out by St Benedict, is that nothing must be set before the worship of God.[2] This is not simply a matter of keeping a strict Rule, it becomes innate that this commerce with God is like breathing. In the safety demonstrations before an airline flight, parents are told that if oxygen masks come down, they must put on their own before helping the children with theirs, for obvious reasons. Religious communities know instinctively that the same principle applies to their own worship – it has the same priority as breathing. There is a practical side to it: just as parents need to ensure their own safety before looking after the needs of the child, lest the child should be left without anyone to help, religious communities' first priority is to make sure of their own standards in prayer before seeking to be of help to anyone else. 'Standards' here is a useful word.

I once visited a German community who had built a new guest house. It was not a large building, but I was struck by how big the guests' rooms were, even though sparsely furnished. I commented to the brother in charge, saying how small our own rooms were at Mirfield by comparison. I was surprised the monastery did not want to get more out of the floor area, given the limitations of their accommodation. His smiling answer to me was, 'we have standards'. That slightly cheeky reply might reflect different national characteristics, but it illustrates the fact that any institution or community worth its salt will have standards: practices and values that are sacrosanct and innate. I was once a guest at a mess dinner in an army establishment and moved to bend under the table to retrieve something – my host quickly restrained me. 'No George – he said with horror – We don't do that.' The formal standards of this dinner expressed something of the dignity of the enterprise in which all were involved: this enterprise was understood to stand higher than the weaknesses and failings of everyone sitting around the table. One final illustration: any visitor to Romania will be struck by the extraordinary generosity of people in receiving visitors – huge spreads on groaning tables by people who often can barely afford it, offered with a humbling zest and cheerfulness. They have standards. It would be unthinkable to do less. Here we have standards that connect up more directly with love for one another, and a high estimation of human dignity, and joyful reverence for the visitor and the stranger.

What are the churches' standards? Church normality-structures have made great advances nowadays on awareness of where people are coming from, and on attuning ourselves and our worship to daily life and people's needs; in many denominations humility about the institution has grown at the expense of dogmatism and judgementalism. We can see high standards on love of neighbour, justice, the common good and on the desire to make worship and belief accessible to people of our culture. There is much here to be proud of. In many countries of the world, including the rich West, social services would be in crisis if the churches ceased their sacrificial work for others. The churches are often the only bodies to speak up when politicians are silent, the only ones to put the searchlight on moral dilemmas which would generally be treated with less thought. In addition, the activity of worship brings people together who would not otherwise experience cooperation and responsibility within a community, and does much to stoke up the fires of hope and joy in a contemporary world where these might otherwise flicker and die. Many church bodies in the West have high standards about ways of making the Church more on-the-ball and vibrant, and enabling people to be confident in themselves and about their faith. All of these reflect high standards that are non-negotiable, and we could add quite a lot more. The churches certainly have standards.

Behind all that, however, lies a shadow-side where some standards have fallen dramatically. Some may point to poor knowledge of the Bible, others to insufficient grasp of what the Christian faith is about, others to the fall in theological ability among many clergy. From a monastic perspective, the most dramatic decline is in prayer and its context. This needs some explaining.

## Prayer and its context

Many people today struggle with prayer, whether lay folk or
clergy, and simply exhorting people to pray is unlikely to help
them much. There is a need to become acquainted with a quintet
of realities that are interlocking in Christian prayer, which are its
necessary context.

1 **Worship:** as a general rule sustained Christian personal prayer
   draws its life from worship together, especially the Eucharist
   and the daily prayers of the Church. Worship can mistakenly
   be seen as the pooling of all the private prayers of the gathered worshippers, when the main flow is in the other direction. It is because of the worship that we are able to pray.
   Of course, there are non-worshippers who pray, one famous
   example being Simone Weil, and there are moments when
   prayer can come spontaneously out of anyone, but in general
   prayer seen as something completely distinct from worship is
   hard to sustain.
2 **Personal prayer:** this is necessary too, if the life of faith is to
   engage with us as persons; we are called to be intimate with
   God and to connect our Christian faith with the inner truth of
   who we are, if it is not to be hollow.
3 **The Church:** prayer with a 'sense of the Church' has already
   been described in Chapter 1. This sense is essential for any who
   want to grow in prayer, or even understand what prayer is,
   and for many it will be a huge encouragement.
4 **The tradition:** there is a massive and rich repertoire on which
   to draw, starting with the Church's ever-evolving traditions
   of daily prayer, and after that the abundant repertoire of
   Christian prayers and writings on prayer. This understanding
   of tradition is incomplete unless held together with worship
   and a 'sense of the Church'.
5 **The world:** Christian prayer reflects the world in which it is set
   and is motivated by it. We all need to be aware of the situation
   of our current world, not least the troubles that plague it. This
   should drive us to prayer if nothing else does. The world needs
   in its midst a Church that is strong, and such a Church can
   only be found if it is a Church that prays.

All these five marks are interlocking – it is difficult to consider one without the others. This is not a test or conundrum to puzzle us, but simply a way of describing what quickly becomes innate in any person who learns to pray within a Church whose life is healthy. These things should need no setting-out – through most of Christian history they have simply been there in the life of the Church, imbibed as if it were our mother's milk. It is a telling indication of our situation that they need spelling out. Hold all five together, and you should be away. Prayer is an absolute standard, like breathing, but it is always felt and breathed as part of an interlocking dance in which the worship of the Christian community is innately there like the foundations of a building, and the whole activity is understood less as a personal quest for support and more as a soul-and-body participation in a great and entrancing reality which is part of the daily life of the whole Church on earth and in heaven, and a living of its forward-flowing tradition, populated by a multitude of people and saints, the Scriptures, truths, dramas, discoveries, visions, books, poets, music, sacrifices, acts of selfless service, an unfinished symphony which simply requires us to pick up our instrument and join in.

## Living with standards

One function of religious communities is to set a plumb line[3] in the midst of the Church – a witness to non-negotiable standards. This does not presume that nuns and monks are exemplary: the plumb line is set alongside them as well. But the 'life' within which religious communities live and work is far greater than the people making it up (participants in a mess dinner understand this). It is a mystery which arches above the particular people trying to live it. The starting point is above us, and to it the people below seek with the help of God to respond, always with failure and sin, and rarely as shining examples. When people express gratitude for what the life and worship of a religious community gives them, every religious community would want to reply that 'it happens despite us'. Monasticism's 'standards' are non-negotiable commitments, the watering-down of which you simply do not do: and they are no mere concepts or ideals but a living reality greater than the people living it.

## Obedience

Normality-structures can only thrive healthily when accompanied by a climate of obedience. No obedience, no normality. What can this mean today, when no one has time for obedience? It is known in the workplace, where employees can be expected to do what they are asked to do, but that is not what we are talking about. There is a distinction between what might be called military obedience and the Christian variety. In the military, an order must be carried out forthwith – it is as simple as that; in the Christian tradition, and especially in monasticism, obedience is to do with mutual listening. The word 'obey' is derived from the word 'listen' in many languages. In Latin, *obaudire* means to listen; in Romanian, the same word, *ascultare*, means both 'listen' and 'obey'; in English, a parent might say 'Why won't you listen to me?', when in fact they mean 'Why won't you obey?'. In St Benedict's Rule for Monks, where obedience is a key to the whole life, the opening word is 'Listen'.

Monastic obedience is a two-way reality: a superior's decisions come from full consultation (St Benedict says: 'always consult, and you will never regret your decisions').[4] He or she needs to know the community member well enough not to ask of them what they cannot do, and needs to be prepared to discuss with the person the request being made to them. For the community member, obedience is seen as sacramental, a place where God is encountered and love of the brethren/sisters is lived out. St Benedict encourages mutual obedience as a characteristic of daily life together, each being quick to take up a task if something needs doing, to give help if it is asked for and to be at the disposal of others.[5] In decision-making processes obedience puts the emphasis on listening, on expecting the other person to say things worth listening to and taking seriously. It is in this context that the superior or another officer is able to ask something with an expectation that it will be done. Obedience affects the way we see each other, treat each other and find God in each other. In other words, it is a frame of mind, a whole approach to life. In distinction from obedience in the army or the workplace, it is lived with a particular sense of relating to something higher. If you like, it is mutual listening to the sound of background music: this 'music' is the eternal song of heaven. It is a fired-up desire to say 'yes', to support the other party in a common response to the love of God. There is a high commitment to pulling together, to giving in order to receive. In the normal run of things, the superior will give the request and the community member will do it – but this is powered not by coercion or inevitability, but by desire, aspiration and love. The foundation of this obedience is identification with Christ's obedience: rather than a mere effort to be obedient, it is a consequence of identification with Jesus, who sought not his own will, but the will of the one who sent him.

Religious communities have no monopoly on this kind of obedience – it is to be found in many enterprises where people work together for a common good, whether religious or not. In the Church, however, it is of the essence of the gospel and applies to all. The challenge is to hold together real freedom of expression and debate, and, where necessary, freedom to protest, with this costly understanding of belonging together as a family whose inner life is God. Holding that balance is not easy, but perfectly do-able. The problem today for the churches is the sheer strength of a secular culture that militates against such obedience and gives a higher value to individual independence of mind and independent action. Both sides of this equation are needed, but the two elements in the contemporary world – and churches – are badly out of balance. This may be seen in a church council meeting where people may get offended or walk out, or press for their own way, or deal with each other adversarially. It can be seen in church governing structures where officers may be subjected to a 'Prime Minister's Question Time' ordeal, rather than offering themselves as fellow-sinners on a mutual quest for the will of God. 'The rulers of the Gentiles lord it over them . . . It will not be so among you' (Matt. 20.25, 26). It can be seen in pick-and-mix approaches to prayer, worship and belief, doing what we feel like, doing what we think we need, rather than sitting under something greater and more demanding. If there are to be standards, then, there has to be a mature sense of Christian obedience.

## Tacit obedience

So far, we have seen obedience to one another as a 'hard listening', a willingness not simply to promote our own views and preferences, but to expect to be changed by what we hear from others, as we become quicker to work and cooperate with them. There is now something else behind all this: a greater listening that can not simply be switched on, but is like a hum in the background, something tacit, akin to what I have called a 'sense of the Church', a tacit awareness of membership of a family that gives us a sense of who we are. It is a tacit obedience that is sufficiently like music for us to take a musical example to illustrate it. I am a not very good organist, but it has sometimes fallen to me to play the organ for all the Holy Week liturgies at Mirfield, and for this a certain amount of improvisation is required – music that is made up as you go along, for accompanying an action. I long ago learnt that in order to improvise tolerably I need in the preceding weeks to play for my own enjoyment as much of the repertoire as I can – organ music from the Renaissance to the present day. My ability to improvise then begins to rise from the ashes and to become, for me at least, something rather exciting. The repertoire has been filling me, and it begins to come out again as I feel my way forward in the improvisations. Creative music-making depends greatly on being formed, shaped, soaked by and in the repertoire.

This phenomenon is familiar in monastic life, and St Benedict insists upon it. For him first of all it means being steeped in the Scriptures. Every page of his Rule for Monks is studded with Bible phrases, often strung together in chains. Religious sisters and brothers in their daily services sit under the word, a strong stream running through every day of their lives. Benedict and the long tradition he represents see this as food to be chewed and digested daily in the practice of *lectio divina*. This means 'holy reading', a practice of reiterative reading-aloud of a passage from Scripture, praying all the while. In its popular modern form a person can spend 30 minutes reading the passage repeatedly with long silences after each reading – it is not Bible study, but a form of prayer in which a voice gradually comes through to us from the word we are 'chewing'.[6]

Secondly for Benedict it means being steeped in the Christian writers,[7] which for us really means the whole gamut of theology and writings on the spiritual life. Both in religious communities and among the clergy it is very difficult today to sustain ongoing study of this kind. There are increased opportunities for laity to study at an academic level, but there is a need for structures that would encourage us all to remain fresh in the Christian repertoire.

Thirdly for Benedict it is about something more mysterious, a tacit awareness, moulded by the tradition that has been passed on, a form of obedience summed up in the Benedictine vow of *conversatio morum*, a notion difficult to put into words, but to do with giving yourself to a whole way of life which has an energy of its own. There are similarities with the organist giving herself to the received tradition of the repertoire, together with a corporate understanding of how it is to be played, so that it may then begin to live in her and speak through her. That giving of self to the organ repertoire requires obedience akin to that of religious brothers and sisters. But what they are trying to do is live the gospel, and therefore this giving of yourself to a living repertoire is something all Christians are called to. In other words, the tacit awareness of the mystery of the Church which we spoke of in Chapter 1 includes trusting the Church and its repertoire to be life-giving, and to let it be a music that is going on in our heads all the time as we go about our lives. It is this 'music' which I am finding myself struggling to speak about in a way that can be grasped, but it lies at the heart of our 'standards'. It is something that becomes part of our grain, a necessary part of any 'sense of the Church', and it is often referred to as the tradition.

## Different vintages of non-obedience

It would not be necessary to struggle to say these things if there were not a problem, present in the different churches in different ways, and already alluded to in Chapter 1. In the Anglican Church it might be put like this (what I describe is also found in the Roman Catholic and other churches but probably not in quite this way). Reports are produced, discussions held, strategies identified, clergy have annual appraisals, parishes are urged to produce audits of areas of their life, and much of this makes complete sense within the terms of its own logic. All of this you would expect in the good running of any organization. But too often it stops there. The enquirer might look in vain for adequate standards on daily prayer set out clearly by the Church's leadership, for instance, or efforts to accompany and support the clergy in it. Very convincing strategies are put forward which make complete sense within their own terms, the financial calculations, the optimum deployment of persons, the rationalizing of structures and systems, the planning of vibrant mission, the quest for joyful confidence. Within their own enclosed order of things, they make complete sense – and yet where is the divine music to be found? Where is the Christian spiritual repertoire of the ages? Where is the sense of the mystery of the Church? Where is the dimension of grace? There seems to be limited ability to stand back from the managing and strategizing in order to appraise them, for it does happen in some cases that managing and strategizing have been nothing less than enthroned. The church-machine needs this tinkering-with to make it work better, and that is that (helped, of course, by the supporting 'resources' of prayer and worship, servicing what are often somewhat human strategies). Beneath it all there is an uncertainty, or lack of confidence, about the relationship between faith and the culture of our society, and an inability to step back and see our society's culture (and the culture of management) from outside. In such a context, all the religious communities can do is quietly and politely to hold something else up, not taking the problem by the scruff of the neck, but simply singing the music for God – and for any who will hear it.

While in Anglicanism some now seem to act in a spirit which shows a loss from sight of the dimension of grace, and a loss of a spirit of deep Christian obedience and listening, giving the greater emphasis to human planning derived from the wisdom of the world, in the Roman Catholic Church two problems with obedience particularly strike the outsider. One, as we have said, is a reliance on top-down control, which universally dampens people's capacity for creativeness and fizz. In the Church at large, there is a climate of having to look over your shoulder, while at the top is a widespread fear of the hurly-burly of greater freedom of speech and action (there have to be parameters – no one would be served well by a church where anything goes – but current parameters are loaded against life that is free). Monastic obedience would suggest a greater degree of mutual listening, of which Pope Francis is showing a patient and persistent example.

Another problem with obedience is seen in the particular shape conservative reaction takes in the Roman Catholic Church, especially about worship. Since the Second Vatican Council, many would agree that important things have been lost. Not only is worship in some places done with insufficient care, banal in its supporting content and too much aimed at the human beings at the expense of the divine mystery, but there is often a strange undermining of the power of the liturgy by a centuries-old legalism, a transactional approach to worship where a main concern is that it should be 'valid', other considerations on quality only following lower down. The now well-established practice of queueing to receive Holy Communion means that many walk away from the priest casually popping a host in their mouth. Here, however, at the moment of communion, is something greater than Moses entering the cloud on Mount Sinai – what happened on Sinai is nothing compared with Christ's gift of himself in the Eucharist in our parish church: it is not enough that the Mass is done and seen to be done – it needs to be celebrated in a way that resonates with the mystery of what God is doing at that moment. It is possible to sympathize with conservative Roman Catholics who feel that the liturgy is not always what it needs to be and something needs to change. The tragedy is that there is often such quick resort to reproducing the forms that immediately preceded Vatican II. There are perhaps three particular reasons for this: a desire for old certainties, a wish to restore a lost sense of reverence, mystery, tradition and beauty, and a lack in the Roman Catholic Church of a strong tradition of conscious, nuanced change, rather than operation by fiat, which is how the dramatic liturgical changes emanating from Vatican II were themselves swept in, not unexpectedly provoking a correspondingly all-or-nothing reaction.

Attempts to reproduce lost certainties never work; in addition, it ought to be clear that people of a different view from this, who believe tradition needs to find expression in a modern idiom, and who see a place for more informal liturgy, are a huge part of the Roman Catholic Church today: this means that calls for a return to the old liturgy and to downgrade Vatican II can only lead to conflict. A deliberate going for conflict is rarely a sign that God is at work. St Benedict speaks of a constant quest for accommodation to reality, rather than the simple implementing of rules.

The urge to reproduce something from the past implies a God who prescribes: the monastic way is not one of prescription, but of finding a workable path, through sustained struggle and listening. Benedict represents this well in his renowned ability to bend the rules in order to meet human weakness halfway. For him it is important to avoid distressing a brother or sister, or by conflict driving them away. The rules serve the lived reality, not vice versa. Differences over worship need to work in the same way, which is the way of Christian obedience.

In this area in the Roman Catholic Church we find not a management culture too defined by the surrounding culture, but an age-old habit of needing to control from above. The question is not an easy one, for the Roman Catholic Church is colossal, the sheer scale of all its organizations daunting to say the least, complicated by every imaginable difference of nationality, culture and point of view. To hold such an organization together, firm structures are undoubtedly needed. However, Pope Francis clearly sees there is room for relaxation – he knows well that too much control from above is as cut off from the dimension of grace as the managerialism of more world-orientated churches; but he is also clearly aware that it takes time to turn a tanker.

The other obvious contribution of monasticism to current debates over worship is liturgical scholarship, again leading in the direction of nuance and flexibility. When monasticism was restored in nineteenth-century France, monks quickly took to studying the texts of the tradition, and these texts showed the tradition to be a living, changing thing. Religious communities as a result were prime movers in that Liturgical Movement which prepared the way for the changes set by Vatican II. They had discovered the importance of the quest for the facts of history, rather than presumed golden ages and golden forms.

## The deeper priorities of the Church

We have taken the Roman Catholic and Anglican churches as working examples, and have referred rather unflatteringly to restricted aspects of their governance, and little to all the riches that are to be celebrated in them, nor to the differences of scale between them, or the fact that the one is child of the other: these comparisons therefore are not commensurate. The difficulties highlighted, on the other hand, are on both sides to do with roots, the sources of the Church's energy and life, and therefore they loom large in our discussion because, if monasticism is about anything, it is about roots and sources. And yet surely, are not all the people who have been criticized in the last few pages striving for the gospel with the best that is in them?

## Striving

For most normal working people the pressure to have a job and a useful path in life is like straining at a leash – you simply have to make sure of it. How can we as Christians ensure that we are always straining at the leash, always striving to give our all? It is easy for the leash to fall slack. In much of his teaching Jesus gives us the carrot or the stick. He often says that in following him we will receive an eternal reward. There is the carrot. With Dives and Lazarus, we have the stick – Dives languishes in torment because of his lack of compassion. Carrots and sticks are a help in our quest to remain people straining at the leash, but they are too crude to get us all the way. The parable of the Good Samaritan and the Beatitudes, for instance, intimate a higher plane that is simply a way of being. Encouragement and threat are only devices on the road towards a greater freedom. Married couples have their carrots and their sticks, but that doesn't make a marriage. Greater than all of that is the mystery that lives in the relationship of two people.

St Benedict too uses both these motivating devices. For instance, he says it is worth our while to work in the Lord's vineyard, for in the end we should be able to enter into his tent and receive our reward. He also uses the stick – he uses excommunication freely, for example, in a way that seems extraordinary to us. Then in the climax of his Rule, Chapter 72 on the good zeal of monks, the motivation becomes corporate, as Benedict brings in the notion of competition.

> This, then, is the good zeal which monks must foster with fervent love: they should each try to be the first to show respect to the other, supporting with the greatest patience one another's weaknesses of body or behaviour, and earnestly competing in obedience to one another . . . Let them prefer nothing whatever to Christ, and may he bring us all together to everlasting life.

Finally, as with Jesus, Benedict comes to a higher way: in Chapter 73 he recommends we read John Cassian – for Cassian this matter is about *compunction*; God puncturing our heart and bringing us to a moment of conversion. Our calling is to daily conversion, and we can expect to revisit time and again that compunction, that piercing of our heart with the divine truth, which is the starting point for Benedict's true zeal.

In the Prologue to his Rule he says, 'let us get up then, at long last, for the Scriptures arouse when they say: it is high time to arise from sleep . . . *Run* while you have the light of life, that the darkness of death may not overtake you.' Later he says, 'we must run and do now what will profit us for ever.' And near the end of it he says again, 'as we progress in this way of life and in faith, we shall run on the path of God's commandments, our hearts overflowing with the inexpressible delight of love.'

It seems strange to talk about monastic life in terms of haste. What we are saying here seems contradictory as well, implying we need to replace *practical* activism with *spiritual* activism. It could seem to say we must try hard to be better, simply using our human resources and our human will *to try hard*. In that last saying of Benedict, near the end of his Rule, he points rather to a higher plane to which by stages we will come, as we discover that our will and our human striving are searched out by God, to be inhabited by him, so that it is God at work in us. This doing, this straining, is graced, the work of the Holy Spirit in us. And so Benedict does not say here that we must run, but that our running will happen, it will simply come about as we progress in the life of faith: 'as we progress in this way of life and in faith, we shall run on the path of God's commandments'. It will be spontaneous. In the end, it is not enough to try hard – we need to allow God into our trying, so that God may guide the steering-wheel with us, and that is something that can only come about when we become less desperate to take everything by the scruff of the neck, and give God the space to come with us in our striving, giving time and space to the dimension of grace.

## The sacrament and those living it

We have been quite critical of fellow-Christians in some of these chapters, while holding up the life of religious communities as an example, and it is important to reiterate here that monastic life is greater than the people who make it up. It is akin to the world of football: the game is one thing, the people who play it another. Bad playing does not reduce the game's potential power to entrance and excite. The lived monastic tradition is a source of grace, but the people who live it would see themselves as patchy exponents of it. They can for instance lose a firm grip on priorities and become over-concerned with the practical running of the institution, and individually they can behave too much as the sinners that they are. Religious sisters and brothers would feel very awkward about being thought a shining example. What is to be held up is the life itself, mysteriously having an effect often despite the people living it. Religious brothers and sisters are more inclined to a penitent humour about themselves, too aware of the frail humanity that marks their lives. Conscious that we are all in the same boat together with general synods and pontifical councils, all religious sisters and brothers can do is politely point out if we think our common boat is leaking.

At the same time, Benedict, as we have seen, does not allow us to stay in our inadequacies. We are called to run after a cluster of prizes, all to do with truth: self-knowledge, discovery of our true selves, discovery of the wonder of others in their own selves, and in all of this the deep abyss of the knowledge of God and God's knowledge of us.

## Waiting

Quantum theory is famous for having discovered that a particle can be a wave at the same time; it can have static position as well as momentum. Parallels are not hard to find in the Christian journey and in the frequent paradoxes in Jesus' teaching. In monastic life, there are similarly strange twinnings of contrary phenomena. One such twinning brings 'running' together with standing stock-still. The monk or nun stands and looks. As one of the sayings of the desert fathers of fourth-century Egypt has it, 'Abba Serapion said, "when the soldiers of the Emperor are standing at attention, they cannot look to the right or left; it is the same for the man who stands before God and looks towards him in fear at all times; he cannot then fear anything from the enemy."' Gilbert Shaw,[8] for some years chaplain of the Sisters of the Love of God in Oxford (and much influenced by Father William of Glasshampton), told the community: 'your work is STANDING – holding things without being deflected by your own desires or the desires of other people around you. Then things work out just through patience. How things alter we don't know, but the situation alters.' This points to a quality of monastic life that is very difficult to describe. It is a refusal, when faced with difficulties, simply to attempt to take them by the scruff of the neck, but instead to endure and wait, often for years or decades. It can be illustrated from the difficulties that inevitably grow up between the members of communities, and works on a basic assumption that God is specially present in the difficulties. There is a story of St Bernard visiting a monastery and finding that all the brothers got on extremely well with each other without any difficulties between them. He told them they needed to recruit some difficult brethren in order to be able to grow in charity with their neighbour, in patience and in self-knowledge. There is no monastic life without struggles over the *difference* among people. Even if we are dealing with one person living alone, unless they are completely cut off from others in strict solitude, there will always be this struggle in relation to others, in which great difficulties may have to be lived with even for decades. This is not a problem to be sorted – it stands near the heart of what the life is about – a working at the coalface of human nature. People are not to be 'sorted' – God is waiting for us in people's intractability. This 'standing' needs endurance, and can lead to misunderstanding and even suffering. Such waiting might at times look like pig-headedness, but it is at the heart of the written tradition, from the desert fathers onwards. This is pretty difficult to understand for our get-up-and-go world, and those responsible for the governance of the churches might think it a recipe for suicide. But the fruits of it are immeasurable. Religious communities have by no means committed suicide. Although they have shrunk in recent years they are lively groups of people, on the whole, and bring up from the depths, almost like a trophy, something that many others struggle to find, although it is there for all.

## Busyness and solitude

This 'trophy' is incredibly eloquent in a world that is busy, noisy and anxious – it is perhaps best expressed in waiting, silence and solitude: the sister or brother every day spends time waiting and attending, being silent in a silent place, and being alone. This habit itself is both the way and the end, the practice is the fruit, as all the variety within us is quietly drawn together in a single focus of oneness. Imprisoned and badgered by a hectic culture, many today sense that this is the calling not only of religious brothers and sisters, but something all of us need to find, in some form or other, if we are to be human beings fully alive.

## Religious communities and the contemporary Church

When anyone visits a religious community or monastic house, whether there be many members or only one, they frequently report finding themselves stopped in their tracks, as dimensions open up that could hardly have been conceived or expected. Numbers of visitors and guests increase all the time, and there is a challenge of finding ways to enable visitors to engage with what lies beneath the surface, for there they will find things that can only but build up the Church and, in a time when many are at a loss, enable it to drink at the sources of the life of the gospel.

### Notes

1 Peter Berger, *The Sacred Canopy*, New York, Anchor, 1967, 1969, pp. 12ff.

2 *Rule of St Benedict* [RB] 43.3.

3 See Amos 7.7–9.

4 *RB* 3.13, quoting Sirach 32.24.

5 See for instance *RB* 72.

6 On chewing the Scriptures, see J. Leclercq, *The Love of Learning and the Desire for God: A Study of Monastic Culture*, New York, Mentor, 1961; London, SPCK, 1978, pp. 89–90.

7 *RB* 73.

8 See Chapter 3, Petà Dunstan in this volume, for more on Gilbert Shaw.

# Afterword

THE RIGHT REVEREND LORD ROWAN
WILLIAMS OF OYSTERMOUTH

It seems to be both dangerous and necessary for us to have heroes, golden ages, lost paradises and so on. Dangerous because we can forget how every human era and every human community is flawed and wounded, and we can create unreal images that encourage us to forget the common lot. But necessary because we need to have a living picture of what our flawed humanity just might look like if some of the more obvious and intrusive of our failures were healed. There is nothing wrong in associating our hopes with great figures or great epochs and cultures: we know our life could be more like that, and that our present mediocrity need not be the last word.

For many Christians, the personality and legacy of Francis of Assisi is the focus of hopes like this. Here, in the middle of a violent, unstable world, was someone who managed to bring new life to the sense of what a life radically shaped by the gospel of Christ would look like. His obstinate simplicity, his capacity to cut through the layers of anxious and self-protective piety to genuine encounter with Christ, his freedom to respond to the entire creation with joy, all these have constantly acted as a reminder to Christians, even those Christians (most of us) who in one way or another shrink from sharing Francis's alarming generosity.

But it is also true that among the 'golden ages' of the Church's history in Britain, the world of early Christianity in the North-East has a special place. That first generation of Northumbrian Christians and their allies and pastors, so lovingly described by the Venerable Bede in his history, has survived in the imagination of many as a moment when the best and most fruitful elements of Celtic and Anglo-Saxon culture were woven together, when the Church was midwife to a wealth of achievement in art and learning, and when something of the same uncluttered, unclouded vision as we see in Francis could be seen in figures like Aidan and Cuthbert; their warmth of heart and simplicity of life were remembered as the cornerstone of Northumbrian Christianity.

The shadows and ambiguities are always there. Francis's last years in the midst of conflicts that nearly tore apart the community he had founded, Bede's lament over the decayed state of the Church in the North-East in his own day, these confirm the fragility of anything that looks like a paradisal era where human sin is suspended. But if the Church is what it says it is, a foretaste of the kingdom of God, we should expect that now and then it will be visible in its true character as a sign of promise – not only in its sacramental life (as is always true) but in specific human biographies and historical movements. Whether in the Church of Aidan and Cuthbert or in the Franciscan experiment, something comes through of the heart of the Church's identity, and it is worth celebrating.

As the essays in this collection make plain, the significance of Shepherds Law has something to do with the particular character of both these historical connections. Here is an enterprise which embodies not only the Franciscan vision but an aspect of that vision which is often overlooked. Francis and many of his followers were as serious about solitude and silence as they were about their engagement with medieval urban society; it was a Franciscan, St Bonaventure, who wrote one of the most comprehensive medieval texts on the contemplative life and the vision of God. As Thomas Merton once observed, the appeal of Franciscan poverty and simplicity would be 'tinny and sentimental' without this deep anchorage in prayer. The hermitage, and Brother Harold's long and costly witness, both speak of this side of Franciscan identity in a way that challenges us to look beyond the popular picture of a saint who was good with animals and children, so to speak, and discover the roots of active compassion in the selflessness of contemplation. It is, of course, associated with a long-standing Franciscan presence in the North-East, which has in its turn looked to the history of the area for inspiration. To unite in this way the legacy of the Northumbrian saints with the

Franciscan ideal is to draw from some very deep wells; and this helps to explain the particular force and significance of Shepherds Law as a presence in the region.

It is, of course, a region all too familiar with economic devastation and a sense of being abandoned by those who make decisions in our country. It is all the more important that there should be a sign – even if it is not known to many in the population at large – of God's fidelity to those living with insecurity and hardship. As Roland Walls and his Community of the Transfiguration demonstrated in their life of extreme poverty and obscurity at Roslin near Edinburgh – another experiment strongly associated with Franciscan tradition – what matters is not publicity and success, but faithful presence, the willingness to be alongside people at their points of hurt and risk. And to do this, as both Roland and his community and Harold have done, from a centre defined by contemplation has demonstrably been as authentic a witness as could be to the nature of God's accompaniment; an equivalent to what Bede describes as typical of the old Northern saints who refused the comforts and safeties of life in order not to be strangers to their struggling neighbours.

It is a witness that the churches of our country badly need. We are prone to worry about the future, hectic activity to develop strategic means of avoiding further decline and so on. There is certainly nothing wicked about planning and reflecting strategically – and once again we need to avoid mythologizing and romanticism; but the most serious question is how we keep open the deepest wells of our Christian life. And this cannot be answered without reference to the experience of those who decide to inhabit the space of silence lived out in Christ, which silences our fear and guilt. To do this with a grateful awareness of those who – like Aidan and Cuthbert – built on that foundation in their own ministry in the past is no less necessary: living consciously and prayerfully in the tradition is stepping into a flowing stream, not shouldering an impossible burden.

This is what Shepherds Law speaks of and why it is timely to reflect on what it is and represents. The essays in this book range from historical to architectural to biographical, but all lead back to the same place: that space and solitude where life in Christ is

uncovered in its full resourcefulness. It is where all the controversy, all the anxiety, all the activism, all the hope and despair
of belonging to a historic church must finally look if they are not
simply to mirror back to the world its own confusion. Thank
God, there are places of clarity. This is one.

# Index of Bible References

# Index of Subjects

CPSIA information can be obtained
at www.ICGtesting.com
Printed in the USA
LVOW12s0448241017
553543LV00004B/302/P